A History of Poland
IN PAINTING

JANUSZ WAŁEK

INTERPRESS PUBLISHERS
WARSAW 1991

Designed by
HUBERT HILSCHER

Translated by
KATARZYNA ZAWADZKA

Historical consultation:
PROFESSOR JANUSZ TAZBIR

Production editor:
ELŻBIETA CHOLERZYŃSKA

Colour reproductions of paintings and drawing by
JERZY MYSZKOWSKI

The remaining colour and black-and-white reproductions by
Mirosław Ciunowicz, Jan Hattowski, Władysław Paweł Jabłoński, Jaworski, Jan Michlewski, Stanisław Michta, Jerzy Nowakowski, Henryk Romanowski, Janusz Rosikoń, Jerzy Sabara, Stanisław Stępniewski, Edward Witecki, Teresa Żółtowska-Huszcza

Black-and-white photographs by courtesy of
Institute of Art of the Polish Academy of Sciences, National Museums in Cracow: Czartoryski Collections, National Library, Maria Curie-Skłodowska Museum, Museum of the History of the Revolutionary Movement, and Central Photographic Agency

On the cover:
Detail of the *The Battle of Grunwald*
by Jan Matejko

On the title page:
View of Cracow with Wawel Castle
from *Civitates orbis terrarum* by Georg Braun,
with illustrations by Franz Hogenberg and Simon Novellanus,
Cologne 1572

A History of Poland in *Painting* appears also in Polish

This is the 2584th book of Interpress

First published 1988

Copyright by Interpress Publishers, Warsaw 1988

ISBN 83-223-2584-3

Printed and bound by Comarex s.r.l., Verona, Italy

List of Contents

The past of the nations is told by pictures and books; pictures and lore handed down by our forefathers. They talk to us from the museum walls and library shelves, they teach us history and enable us to look into the mysterious well of time. Many of such documents were lost, swallowed up by wars, occupations, uprisings and other historical turmoil. The losses in Polish culture are enormous, amounting to thousands of books and thousands of paintings. Flames bit into the panels and canvas of many a painting which commemorated the features of outstanding men and their deeds. The song was more difficult to kill; retained in memory, it resisted longer and more successfully. It was handed down from generation to generation by word of mouth, circulating in handwritten copies.

A picture of past centuries as seen by the poet and the painter is a fascinating one. It is not a mere document: an important role is played here by the author's personality, the intention of the patron who commissioned a picture or a poem, current propaganda needs, and numerous other reasons. The poems and pictures therefore reflect moods, and nuances of human attitudes.

Painting had existed long before man learned how to write. Touching images of primeval man have survived on the rocky walls of caves in France, Spain and Africa. With just a few strokes and a combination of colour patches of astonishing finery, the palaeolithic artist recorded man's combat against the forces of Nature, his struggle for survival in which early social relations were formed. The word has not come down to us from that time long buried in the past; neither the words of those early songs which coordinated the rhythm of joint labour, nor those which with time helped to consolidate family and tribal ties. The echoes of these early rhymes can be discerned in the songs of sailors, harvesters and weavers, who, in the present epoch of tape recorders, have unfortunately fallen silent.

It was these songs that gave rise to first great literary works, the epic poems of the kind Homer wrote.

In book xviii of the *Iliad* Homer gives a magnificent imaginary description of Achilles' shield, the work of Greek armourers, which is emblazoned with a representation of a battle waged before the walls of a town:

"Leaving debate undecided they mounted at once on their war-steed,
— High-stepping steeds were they — and hastily throng'd to combat.
So was the battle join'd, and the armies fought by the stream-side.
E'en on the river's bank; and they aim'd at each other with sharp spears.
Tumult and Strife were there. — Fate, also, was busy among them,
Dragging away one man with a recent wound, and another
Yet unwounded: — a corpse she had seized on, holding the ankles.
Crimson, with human gore, was the tint of her terrible garment.
Like unto living men, on the shield, were the forms of fighters;
One might have seen them draw each other the prize of the corpses."

The shield of Achilles also featured scenes of peaceful life:

"Reapers, reaping the crop with the bright hooks grasp'd in their right hands.
Here of the sever'd ears were the full swaths tumbling earthwards:

9

Others, the binders of sheaves were collecting and binding in bundles:
Three were in number the binders; and, joyfully thronging behind them,
Children gather'd the corn and carried it onwards in armfuls;
Bringing an ample supply to be bound..."*

The arts and literature offer a rich picture of everyday life in the past. Thanks to works of art we know how people dressed in the past, what the interiors of their homes looked like, how they worked, enjoyed themselves, how they travelled and how they fought. The arts and literature constitute an inestimable source of information on the past historical epochs.

In Polish culture, an equivalent, as it were, of the shield described by Homer is the Gniezno Door, a magnificent 12th century monument consisting of a number of sculpted scenes depicting St. Adalbert's historical mission in Prussia at the time of Boleslaus the Brave. This work, as well as the surviving stone tympana in Romanesque churches (they show the first portraits of real people, i.e. church founders), provide us with a picture of people and events concerning the beginnings of the Polish state. This picture is complemented with early literary texts, such as the 12th century chronicle of Gallus Anonymous, the first recorded history from the earliest, legendary times till the reign of Boleslaus Wrymouth.

These are chiefly fantasy rather than documents, although we succumb to their power and readily regard them as credible.

On the walls of the Athenian Stoa Poikile the painter Panaios, nephew of the great Phidias, commemorated the battle between the Greeks and Persians at Marathon. The painting, no longer in existence, was for generations of Athenians a memento of an important event in their history and an inspiring lesson in patriotism.

An important aspect of painting and literature dealing with historical themes is to bring home to the nation its past, to recall in difficult moments its past glory and to set ideals to imitate. Especially in Poland the arts have often played this role.

One of the earliest examples of historical painting in Poland, *The Battle of Orsza* (National Museum in Warsaw) dates back to the early 16th century. It has been established that this painting was not a unique specimen. At that time there existed other historical representations, too, including wall paintings (another *Battle of Orsza* and *Battle against the Tartars at Wiśniowiec* at the Franciscan monastery in Cracow), but they were destroyed. Not much has survived from the later period either (among other things the series of paintings presenting the story of Maryna Mniszech, a series of twelve paintings from Tyniec — now in the convent at Staniątki — and a number of works from the days of John III commemorating his military successes). However it was not until the end of the 18th century that the historical genre was initiated by the last king of Poland, Stanislaus Augustus Poniatowski, who commissioned the Italian Marcello Bacciarelli to paint episodes of Polish history to serve as the decoration of the Knights' Hall at the Royal Castle in Warsaw.

Almost simultaneously the events connected with the death agony of the Polish Commonwealth — the dramatic Four Year Seym, the proclamation of the Constitution of 3rd May, the Kosciuszko Insurrection — made the artists take to the streets and battlefields where they (Norblin, Orłowski) did quick sketches, pictorial reports as it were, of such scenes as the hanging of the Targowica traitors in Warsaw, and the peasant scythebearers storming of the enemy cannon at Racławice.

The 19th century witnessed the heyday of historical painting. The studios of many artists (January Suchodolski, Leopold Loeffler, Józef Brandt and Wojciech Gerson,

---

* Both quotations come from *The Iliad* of Homer in English Hexameter Verse by J. Henry Dort, M.A. of Exeter College, Oxford, London, Longmans, Green and Co MDCCCIXV

to mention but a few) were converted into rich storehouses of arms, clothes, stuffed horses and old folios in which attractive anecdotes were sought. Jan Matejko, undoubtedly the most eminent of them all, was inspired by the historian Jan Długosz's *Historia Polonica* (1455—80) when he painted in 1878 *The Battle of Grunwald,* a masterpiece among battle scenes in Polish and foreign painting.

Let us compare these two renditions of the famous battle: the literary presentation which originated some decades after the event, and the pictorial one executed some five centuries later.

"Warrior pushed warrior, weapons broke with crash, arrows aimed at faces. In all this commotion and hubbub it was difficult to make out the brave ones from the chicken-hearted, for they all were suspended in one crowd."

In Matejko' painting too all are "suspended in one crowd". The knights, horses, lances, swords and banners swirl around the motionless, calm Grand Duke Witold, who perhaps personifies the triumph of the good and just over the evil and wrong done to nations.

The painter's vision of the victory over the aggressive Germanic element was included in the treasury of national art in the gloomy period — at that time lasting already some decades — of political bondage, and for the contemporaries its significance was not of purely artistic nature. During World War II the significance of this painting was well understood of the Nazis who searched for the painting, which had been hidden by the Poles, as if it were a dangerous criminal.

In artistic creations — especially poetry and painting — there is a strength which dry documents sometimes lack. Art appeals more strongly to imagination, attacks emotions in a more powerful way and leaves its indelible imprint on the memory. Could we find words which would better reflect the echoes of particular political moods than those of *La Marseillaise* or the *Dąbrowski Mazurka*? Would it be possible to better express the enthusiasm of revolution or the tragedy of aggressive war than did Delacroix in his *Liberty Guiding the People* or Goya in the *Execution of the Defenders of Madrid?*

But painting and literature dealing with historical themes are significant for other reasons, too; they constitute an attempt to find in history the reasons for national disasters, analyze shortcomings and sins, and reflect on the national conscience.

Schlegel once called a historian "a prophet turned towards the past" (*einen rückwärts gekehrten Propheten*), and a good, genuine artist who uses history as his working material is exactly such a prophet. Matejko and Wyspiański, perhaps just those two, were prophets of this kind in Polish art. Their oeuvre is addressed to the present day: they condemn the errors made in the past and warn against making new ones. It it their creative criticism that is most precious. And here we come upon the problem of the great responsibility of the artist whose art deals with historical and national themes.

Today, towards the end of the 20th century, when yesterday's happenings take on an historical dimension, the arts seem unable to keep pace. They seem to be ousted by photography, film and sound recordings, collected in huge archives. Yet the artist keeps vigil; he looks on, ponders, and creates new works in the idiom of contemporary poetry and painting, not immediately understood by everybody, but which eventually becomes the common good. A case in point here is Picasso's *Guernica,* the famous picture commemorating the civil war in Spain — another picture sign, another example of the artist's moral duty towards history and the present day. A warning sign of the artist and patriot.

The selection of pictures by Polish painters entitled *A History of Poland in Painting* is not a history textbook. It is not a document of historical events, either. It is a picture of historical events as the artists saw them. It is an imaginary picture of the past, usually painted some time after the event portrayed took place. Sometimes so many years had passed that it refers more to the times when it was executed rather than to the actual event of the past it depicts. Such is the case with Jan Matejko whose great analytical compositions tell us more about the people and the moods of the second half of the 19th century than about the more distant past.

The picture of Poland's history presented here comprises works of varying artistic merit. Outstanding works can be found side by side with mediocre, primitive ones. But these inferior paintings did play their role, particularly in the 19th century, at the time of the partitions, when they were extremely popular. It was thanks to these paintings that archetypes of struggles, victories, bondage, and defeats still linger on in the public imagination.

Thus the picture of Polish history is diversified, rich and fascinating with a multitude of genres and styles. It is many-hued, although alas light and bright colours are not in abundance; gloomy and sombre ones prevail. Blood and tears often appear on the palette of the Polish artist.

The paintings collected in this book do not illustrate all events and do not record all historical figures, nor do they deal with all the problems. They are concerned only with the events, people and problems taken notice of, selected and appreciated — sometimes overestimated — by the artists.

It is chiefly paintings that are presented here. Sculpture and things like fabrics, which have also featured historical themes, are left out; only a few prints and drawings are reproduced and just one poster.

The author feels obliged to add that the task of collecting this material was facilitated by his participation in work connected with *Polish Self-portrait,* an exhibition organized in 1979 at the National Museum in Cracow by a team headed by Marek Rostworowski.

Moreover, thanks are due to Professor Janusz Tazbir for numerous expert comments and helpful corrections, as well as to Mrs. Ewa Trzeciak, the editor of the Polish version, for her many creative suggestions and patience shown throughout the whole period of preparing this book.

KORNELI SZLEGEL (1819—70)

Pilgrims Visiting Piast

NATIONAL MUSEUM IN CRACOW

According to an ancient legend,
recorded by Gallus Anonymous, the
author of the oldest (12th century)
Polish chronicle, the Polish royal line
originated from peasant stock in
a humble wheelwright called Piast.
His descendants were Ziemowit,
Lestko, Siemiomysł, and, finally, prince

Mieszko I, who won fame in lengthy
wars with the Germans and
adopted Christianity in 966, the
year which marks the beginning of
the first historical dynasty ruling in
Poland.

The Piast dynasty came to an
end when Casimir the Great died
without issue in 1370.

This sentimental painting by Korneli
Szlegel shows the Angels who
appeared at Piast's farmstead to tell
him that he had an important mission
to fulfil.

13

ALEKSANDER LESSER (1814—84)

The Death of Wanda

NATIONAL MUSEUM IN WARSAW

"... So greatly did she overshadow all the others with her beautiful form and alluring charms that you might have thought that Nature, when bestowing these gifts upon her, was not only generous but prodigal. For even the most prudent among the enemy mellowed at the sight of her." This is how the legendary princess Wanda of Cracow was described by Master Wincenty Kadłubek (c. 1150—1223), Bishop of Cracow, and author of a chronicle recording the history of Poland from the earliest times till the beginning of the 13th century.

With the passage of time the legend of Wanda, daughter of Prince Krak, the founder of Cracow, high priestess and queen to the Vandal people settled on the river Vandalus, that is, the Vistula, acquired new elements. According to one of them, Wanda refused a German prince called Rytgier who was seeking her hand in marriage. The latter, thirsting for vengeance, took up arms against the Vandal people, and in order to save her subjects Wanda threw herself into the river.

In the 19th century, the death of Wanda "who didn't want a German for a husband" joined the permanent repertoire of patriotic songs and poems, and also became a frequent subject of drawings and paintings, among which the painting by Lesser is one of the most popular.

14

JAN MATEJKO (1838—93)

Introduction of Christianity in Poland from the series The History of Civilization in Poland

NATIONAL MUSEUM IN WARSAW

The greatest Polish national painter, Jan Matejko, produced this series of twelve sketches entitled *The History of Civilization in Poland* in 1888 and 1889, just a few years before his death. This series gives a survey of the most important events in Polish history from the introduction of Christianity in 966 until the time of the partitions as a result of which towards the end of the 18th century Poland lost independence for more than a hundred years.

Among the other momentous events Matejko commemorated is the coronation of Boleslaus the Brave as the first king of Poland, the founding of the university in Cracow by Casimir the Great, the baptism of Lithuania, the first royal election in Poland, and the proclamation of the May 3rd Constitution. The artist paid special attention to the evolution of state and civil law in Poland, and to the development of education and culture, especially during the 16th century — the spectacular Jagiellonian "golden age".

The paintings were supplemented with a printed commentary written by Matejko himself — something very unusual for an artist who was generally very reticent about his work — which testifies to the importance he attached to these sketches.

The Introduction of Christianity in Poland, which opens the series, is a somewhat theatrical scene set on the bank of Lednica Lake in Great Poland. It depicts the apostle of the Christian faith in Poland and the first patron saint of Poland, St. Adalbert, together with Prince Mieszko I, his future wife, the Czech princess Dubrava, and Benedictine monks. The latter, coming to Poland from the West, brought with them to the pagan country both the new faith and advanced western civilization. New methods of land tilling and building, and new customs, quickly — though not without obstacles — caught on in Poland which through accepting Christianity from Rome entered for good the orbit of western civilization. The adoption of Christianity was of enormous importance for the young Slav state, for it removed the danger of aggression by the Holy Roman Empire which used the aim of converting the pagan Slavs to Christianity as an excuse to expand its political influence.

MICHAŁ BYLINA (1904—82)

Boleslaus the Brave and His Retainers on the Baltic

POLISH ARMY MUSEUM IN WARSAW

The reign of Boleslaus the Brave, the first of the great Polish kings (crowned in 1025), which abounded in military campaigns conducted in the eastern and western areas of Poland, saw the consolidation of the young Piast country which now extended well beyond its ethnic frontiers (dating from the period of Mieszko I). Of immense political and economic importance was the access to the sea secured by Boleslaus the Brave with the setting up of a Polish bishopric in Kołobrzeg in 1000. Although later Poland lost influence there, the fight for the restoration of Polish sovereignty over Pomerania was continued by Boleslaus the Brave's successors (including Boleslaus Wrymouth) for many centuries. Finally, in 1945 Poles returned to Pomerania and the ceremonial reunion with the Baltic took place in Kołobrzeg.

Boleslaus the Brave (967—1025), called Boleslaus the Great by Gallus Anonymous, waged numerous victorious wars, the aim of which was in part to free Poland from the German empire and to strengthen the frontiers of the state. This in Boleslaus' times covered a major area in Europe, stretching from the Baltic in the North to the Tatra mountains in the South and from the Elbe in the West to the Bug in the East. Paweł Jasienica wrote that "the epoch of Boleslaus the Brave gave the nation a feeling of its own worth".
Detail of a drawing by Jan Matejko (1838—93) from a series *Portraits of Polish Kings and Princes* (1890—92)

PIOTR MICHAŁOWSKI (1800—55)

Boleslaus the Brave Entering Kiev

NATIONAL MUSEUM IN WARSAW

Boleslaus the Brave who — as mentioned before — conducted wars both in the West and in the East, became involved in the affairs of his son-in-law Sviatopluk. In an attempt to place Sviatopluk on the throne of Kiev he stormed the town, captured it in 1018 and annexed the Czerwieńsk Strongholds to Poland (they returned to Kiev Rus in 1031). This marked the beginning of Poland's wars in the eastern regions, which were not always conducted to her advantage.

Tradition has it *(Great Poland Chronicle)* that on entering Kiev Boleslaus the Brave struck the Golden Gate with his sword making a jag in the metal. The famous Jagged Sword ("Szczerbiec") which is today in the collection of the Wawel Castle and which was the coronation sword of the kings of Poland, used for the first time at the coronation of Ladislaus the Short in 1320, is however a later copy, produced in the 12th or 13th century.

This painting evoking early Polish history is rather unusual for this most outstanding of Polish Romantic painters, excellent portraitist, illustrator of the Napoleonic legend. However it testifies to the artist's great skill, not least as a colourist.

CIRCLE OF THE MASTER OF THE LEGEND OF ST. JOHN THE
ALMONER (EARLY 16TH CENT.)

Punishment of Unfaithful Wives

STATE ART COLLECTIONS AT WAWEL, PIESKOWA SKAŁA CASTLE

This panel of the triptych from
Cracow's Church on the Cliff is
a rare example of an historical theme
in Polish painting dating from the turn
of the Middle Ages and the
Renaissance.

The panel (c. 1500) reconstructs an event
which took place in the 11th century:
King Boleslaus the Bold passing
a harsh sentence upon the wives of
his soldiers, who were unfaithful to
their husbands while the latter were
away on a military expedition. On the
king's order the women are to suckle
puppies, while their own children —
born out of wedlock — are suckled
by bitches.

The painting also shows Bishop
Stanislaus Szczepanowski — later
a saint and patron of Poland —
reproaching the king for his cruelty.
Bishop Szczepanowski suffered
death by order of the king
in 1079, in rather obscure circumstances
perhaps connected with the
bishop's alleged participation in a plot
against the king.

19

UNKNOWN ARTIST (14TH CENT.)

**Battle of Legnica
The Death of Henry
the Pious at the Battle
of Legnica
miniatures in the so-called
Legend of St. Jadwiga
(Hedvig) of Silesia**

The battle waged on 9 April 1241 on the fields of Legnica, by the Silesian and Great Polish knights against the Tartars, though it ended in the latter's victory, checked the thus far uncontrolled westward expansion of the Asiatic peoples.

Many illustrious knights and princes of the West died in the battle, including their commander Henry the Pious (1191—1242), Prince of Silesia, Great Poland and Cracow, who had made several attempts at uniting sections of the disintegrated country and re-establishing a strong kingdom of Poland.

An illustration taken from the mediaeval legend of St. Jadwiga (Hedwig) of Silesia (Henry's mother, worshipped as the patroness of Silesia) depicts a cruel scene of the severed head of the prince stuck on

a spear being carried round the walls of the town besieged by Tartar hordes.

The battle of Legnica was later to become a frequent subject for artists.

This theme was also taken up by Jan Matejko in his series *The History of Civilization in Poland* in which the artist portrayed not the battle itself, but the solemn funeral, full of grief and intensity, of the fallen princes at Wrocław cathedral. "Through suffering defeat and pain, the nation was reborn and gained a new strength which it had lacked up till then," wrote the artist in the commentary on the painting addressed to his contemporaries, the enslaved Poles of the 19th century.

The haunting spectacle of Prince Henry falling to his death after a mortal blow, was evoked by Stanisław Wyspiański in one of his finest designs for stained glass. The image of the prince bathed in the fiery glow of blood was to have been placed in a window of Wawel Cathedral, next to striking funebral portraits of Bishop Stanislaus Szczepanowski and King Casimir the Great. Alas, these projects were not carried out.

MAKSYMILIAN GIERYMSKI (1846—74)

Skirmish with the Tartars

MUSEUM OF ART IN ŁÓDŹ

For the population living on the margins of the former Commonwealth the threat of Tartar raids was a constant source of terror which continued for several centuries. Bringing with them death and conflagration, the astonishingly dexterous hordes thundering through on their agile horses ravaged a large part of Poland during the 13th century, reaching as far west as Legnica and thereby becoming a serious threat to Western Europe.

Polish knights were later to take part in numerous retaliatory actions (including the one at Wiśniowiec in 1514).

In the 17th century, Tartar forces, then under Turkish influence, sometimes sided with Poland, for example in the Polish-Swedish wars.

22

WOJCIECH GERSON (1831—1901)
The Death of Przemysł
NATIONAL MUSEUM IN WARSAW

At the time of feudal disintegration, Przemysł II, Piast prince of Great Poland, had perhaps the greatest chance of uniting the Polish lands, and actually assumed the royal title in 1295. During an attempt to secure free access to the Baltic for Poland he regained Pomerania and Gdańsk, conquered earlier by Boleslaus Wrymouth and then lost; this encountered strong opposition on the part of the margraves of Brandenburg.

The great Polish families of Nałęcz and Zaręba did not approve of the growing power of Przemysł, either. And so on 8 February 1295 at Rogoźno, the Germans with the help of native firebrands murdered the king, thereby for a time putting an end to the idea of unification. The task of reunion was to be effectively undertaken by Przemysł's successor Ladislaus the Short.

The subject of the murder of the ruler was also taken up by Jan Matejko in one of his less well-known pictures.

23

JAN MATEJKO (1838—93)

Ladislaus the Short Breaking off Agreements with the Teutonic Knights at Brześć Kujawski

NATIONAL MUSEUM IN WARSAW

The motif of the Teutonic Knights often appears in Polish painting and literature and finds its full expression in the *Battle of Grunwald* by Jan Matejko and the novel *The Teutonic Knights* by Henryk Sienkiewicz. The past of the two neighbouring peoples, the Germans and the Slavs, abounds in painful events, strife and armed conflicts.

The Knights of the German Order (Deutscher Orden), known in Poland as the Knights of the Cross because of the black crosses adorning their white cloaks, were invited to Poland in 1226 by Prince Conrad of Masovia who saw in them useful allies in his struggle to subjugate pagan Prussia. He did not realize that this step might give rise to Polish-German conflicts which would go on for many centuries and come to an end as late as World War II.

Ladislaus the Short (1260—1333), crowned king of Poland in 1320, in an attempt to unite the disintegrated state, waged war against the Teutonic Knights first of all in order to regain Pomerania which had been lost in 1308. Despite the victorious battle of Płowce in 1331 these efforts did not bring the hoped for results.

This less well-known picture by Jan Matejko shows one of the many episodes in these long struggles. At the congress in Brześć Kujawski, King Ladislaus the Short is shown breaking off agreements with the Order of the Teutonic Knights represented by the Master John of Lützenburg.

24

RAFAŁ HADZIEWICZ (1803—86)

Casimir the Great
Granting Privileges to the Peasants

NATIONAL MUSEUM IN WROCŁAW

Casimir the Great's kindness to the peasant estate was legendary. "The Peasant King", as he was sometimes called (cf. the popular novel by Józef Ignacy Kraszewski) "loved them [the peasants] very much, liked to talk to them, asking them how they were and how their lords treated them. He readily defended them and punished anybody who did them harm" — thus is described the last Piast king in a popular outline history of Poland published in the early 20th century (Julian Baczyński).

The king — an engineer of internal order in Poland, reformer of the army, economy and education — having carried out the great task of codifying the laws (Wiślica-Piotrków Statutes), indeed tried to protect the peasants from the licence of their lords. However the laws passed at the time of Casimir the Great limited the possibilities for peasants of free movement, which in time made them virtually slaves at the places where they were to perform their obligatory labour dues.

WOJCIECH GERSON (1831—1901)

Casimir the Great and the Jews

NATIONAL MUSEUM IN WARSAW

The Jews began to settle in Poland as early as the 13th century and found favourable living conditions there. The influx of Jews increased in the 14th century, during the period of persecution they suffered in other European countries. Religious tolerance, the pride of Poland at that time, made it possible for the Jews to practice their religion, freely build synagogues and cultivate their customs.

The Jews were greatly indebted to King Casimir the Great (1310—70) who on three occasions — in 1334, 1354, and 1367 — proclaimed laws and privileges regulating the status of Jewry. Casimir's laws guaranteed their personal security and defined the jobs they were free to perform, including those connected with trade (on an equal footing with the burghers), banking, crafts, and the leasing of inns and mills from the nobility.

The Jews have had a permanent place in the political, cultural and economic life of Poland, in which they often played an important role. On several occasions they joined with the Poles in the defence of their common fatherland.

Casimir the Great (1310—70), the last of the Piasts to occupy the Polish throne, "ordered the country internally by reason of his wisdom and understanding" (Jan Długosz). It was his achievement to create a solid state structure, develop military potential, and introduce social order through the establishment of just laws and institutions which guaranteed a life in peace, and to set up the first institution of higher education in Poland: the Cracow Academy.
Detail of tombstone in Wawel Cathedral (1379—80)

BRONISŁAW ABRAMOWICZ
(1837—1912)

Feast at Wierzynek's

NATIONAL MUSEUM IN CRACOW

In January 1363, on the occasion of the wedding of the Emperor Charles IV of Luxemburg and Casimir the Great's grand-daughter Elizabeth, a distinguished assembly of European royalty and princes arrived in Cracow. Among those present were Louis, King of Hungary, Pierre de Lusignan, King of Cyprus, Valdemar, King of Denmark, Otto, Prince of Bavaria, the Silesian princes Boleslaus of Świdnica and Ladislaus of Opole; and the bride's father, the Pomeranian prince, Boguslaus. The wedding ceremonies in the beautiful and prosperous Gothic town of Cracow lasted for twenty days. Numerous feasts, jousting tournaments,

28

and disputes provided the opportunity and the background for the consolidation of a political alliance against the imminent Turkish threat.

Mikołaj Wierzynek, the general steward of the royal court and treasury, Cracow merchant, banker and councillor, gave at that time — at the expense of the council — a feast for Casimir's guests, which went down in history for its sumptuousness. This, undoubtedly the most splendid banquet ever to be held in Cracow, was long remembered for the opulent array of gold crowns, silk, magnificent tableware and for the dazzling gifts (worth some 100,000 ducats) bestowed by Wierzynek on his guests.

On the basis of a museum storehouse of tableware and costumes the academic painter Bronisław Abramowicz executed an interesting, though perhaps too theatrical and formal, picture. The august retinue of guests entering Wierzynek's home (now Cracow's most elegant restaurant) was also painted by Jan Matejko.

JÓZEF SIMMLER (1823—68)

Queen Jadwiga's Oath

NATIONAL MUSEUM IN WARSAW

The painting by Simmler depicts the scene of the oath sworn by Queen Jadwiga (Hedvig) accused of adultery by a certain Gniewosz of Dalewice. This little known episode probably taken from Karol Szajnocha's book *Jadwiga i Jagiełło* points to the continuous dependence of the private lives of public figures on various influences, pressures and intrigues, which more often than not have a political background.

Jadwiga (c. 1374—99), the younger daughter of Louis d'Anjou of Hungary who ruled in Poland after the death of Casimir the Great, from 1384 the Queen of Poland, was married in 1386 at the age of eleven to Ladislaus Jagiello almost three times her age, though she had been betrothed since infancy to William of Habsburg. The Austrians pinned their hopes on this marriage and William used to come to Cracow before Queen Jadwiga married Jagiello and had met her secretly at the Franciscan monastery. William was refused Jadwiga's hand in marriage because political considerations favoured an alliance with Lithuania which could be well served by her marriage with Jagiello.

The court intrigue — the subject of Simmler's painting — took place in 1387. The old man holding the Bible before the Queen is Jaśko of Tęczyn, castellan of Wojnicz; behind him is the false accuser Gniewosz of Dalewice, and Jagiello can be seen standing on the right.

MARCELLO BACCIARELLI (1731—1818)

Ladislaus Jagiello Granting Privileges to the Cracow Academy

NATIONAL MUSEUM IN WARSAW

The oldest Polish university, the Cracow Academy (since the second half of the 19th century known as the Jagiellonian University) was founded by Casimir the Great in 1364. After a period of stagnation following the death of the king, the act of foundation was renewed on 26 July 1400 by Ladislaus Jagiello. Jagiello bequeathed Queen Jadwiga's (d. 1399) entire personal fortune, including jewelry, for the refounding of the Cracow Academy and granted the school special privileges whereby it was to own villages, salt mines and landed estates, the revenues going to its needs.

Soon the Cracow university was to gain fame in Europe for its high standards of scholarship and illustrious graduates, including Nicolaus Copernicus and Andrzej Frycz Modrzewski.

The painting by Bacciarelli recording the event was one of a series of historical paintings commissioned by King Stanislaus Augustus for the Royal Castle in Warsaw.

JAN MATEJKO (1838—93)

Battle of Grunwald, detail

NATIONAL MUSEUM IN WARSAW

On 15 July 1410 on the fields of Grunwald, a battle was waged in which the combined Polish-Lithuanian-Ruthenian forces under the Polish king Ladislaus Jagiello won a splendid victory over the Teutonic army. The victory marked the beginning of the gradual decline of the Teutonic power which had been threatening the freedom and peace of the nations inhabiting the eastern territories of Europe.

The battle scene by Matejko reveals his unrivalled mastery of the medium. It is, as it were, a cross-section through a swirling mass of knights and horses intertwined in mortal struggle. Some characters however are brought into relief, for example the Grand Master Ulrik von Jungingen charged by two Lithuanian peasants. It is not by accident that they attack the Grand Master with St. Maurice's spear (a gift from the Emperor Otto III for Boleslaus the Brave) and that one of them is wearing the red hood of a hangman, for they are engaged not so much in a struggle as in the execution of a death sentence on

the hateful foe. The painting brings to mind a folk tale in which the good and the just get the upper hand over the evil and the unjust. This impression is further augmented by the monumental representation of Grand Duke Witold (Vitautas) galloping straight for the spectator, with his sword raised ready to deal the final blow.

Within this battling mass the Bohemian knight Jan Ziška and the famous Zawisza Czarny (The Black Knight) can be discerned, and in the background, on top of a hillock Jagiello's position being attacked by a German rider.

33

Ladislaus Jagiello (1348—1434), Grand Duke of Lithuania, king of Poland (crowned in 1386), founder of the Jagiellonian dynasty, conqueror of the Teutonic Knights at the battle of Grunwald.

This alleged likeness of the king comes from a section of a triptych by the Master of Our Lady of Sorrow (c. 1470—80) at Wawel Cathedral

ŁUKASZ EWERT

Triumphant Procession of Casimir the Jagiellonian after Capturing Malbork

NATIONAL MUSEUM IN GDAŃSK

Gdańsk, which from 1308 had been in the hands of the Teutonic Knights, shook off this yoke by starting an uprising in 1454. The patricians of the Pomeranian towns — Gdańsk, Elbląg, Toruń and Grudziądz — turned for help to Casimir the Jagiellonian (1427—92), the king of Poland, who on 22 February 1454 declared war on the Order. Thus began the Thirteen Years' War which ended with Poland's victory sealed by the Peace of Toruń (1466), whereby Poland regained access to the Baltic and strengthened its ties with Gdańsk. The Gdańsk burghers gave an enthusiastic welcome to Casimir the Jagiellonian in May 1457 and were in turn granted numerous privileges.

The painting from Arthur's Court in Gdańsk depicting the burghers of Gdańsk following the king's carriage refers to the siege and capture of Malbork by the Polish army in 1460, an accomplishment in which Gdańsk detachments had their share.

UNKNOWN ARTIST

**Stall-holders
Tailor's Shop
miniatures from
Balthasar Behem's Codex**

JAGIELLONIAN LIBRARY IN CRACOW

Completed in 1505 by the
municipal scribe Balthasar Behem,
the Codex containing the statutes of
artisan guilds in Cracow was adorned
with 27 colour miniatures. These
miniatures portray bell founders,
tailors, armourers, painters, and other
artisans at work, usually in their own
workshops, as well as streets with stalls
and pedlars, giving a broad survey
of urban life in the early 16th century.
The realism employed in depicting
human faces and the attention paid
to detail are truly amazing: here we
have the realities of everyday life,
clothing and objects, as well as
sweeping — though largely
conventional — landscapes.

38

UNKNOWN ARTIST
King after the Coronation Ceremony miniature from Erazm Ciołek's Pontifical
NATIONAL MUSEUM IN CRACOW, CZARTORYSKI LIBRARY

Whereas the splendid miniatures in Balthasar Behem's Codex depict the everyday atmosphere of merchant and artisan Cracow at the turn of the Middle Ages and the Renaissance, the somewhat later (c. 1515) Pontifical (that is, the bishop's codex, comprising a collection of rules on liturgical rites performed by bishops) of Erazm Ciołek introduces us to such great ecclesiastical ceremonies as the consecrations of bishops or royal coronations. These magnificent ceremonies were truly worthy of the capital town of Cracow which was then at the peak of its spectacular development.

UNKNOWN ARTIST

The King at the Seym
woodcut from the so-called Laski Statute

As shown in an illustration for Jan Laski's treatise of 1506, Poland is a model, law abiding, constitutional state in which power is wielded by the king dependent in his decisions on the senate and all the nobility. King Alexander (I) the Jagiellon is portrayed at the Seym against the background of shields emblazoned with the coats-of-arms of Polish lands and fiefdoms. It was King Alexander who endorsed the privileges granted to the nobility and promised them that *nihil novi* (nothing new) would be moved without the consent of the Seym.

Chancellor Jan Laski (1455—1531) is handing the king the sealed parchment containing the text of the Nihil Novi Constitution which confirms the golden freedom of the nobility. The law — protecting the subjects from the absolutism of the ruler — would later foment anarchy among the nobility, which paralyzed the effective government of the country and, in turn, became one of the chief causes of the political disaster in the 18th century.

Nicolaus Copernicus (1473—1543), student of the Cracow Academy, greatest Polish scholar, astronomer, author of *De Revolutionibus orbium coelestium* (1543), the work which revolutionized ideas on man and the world.
Portrait by an unknown painter of the first quarter of the 16th century, Regional Museum in Toruń

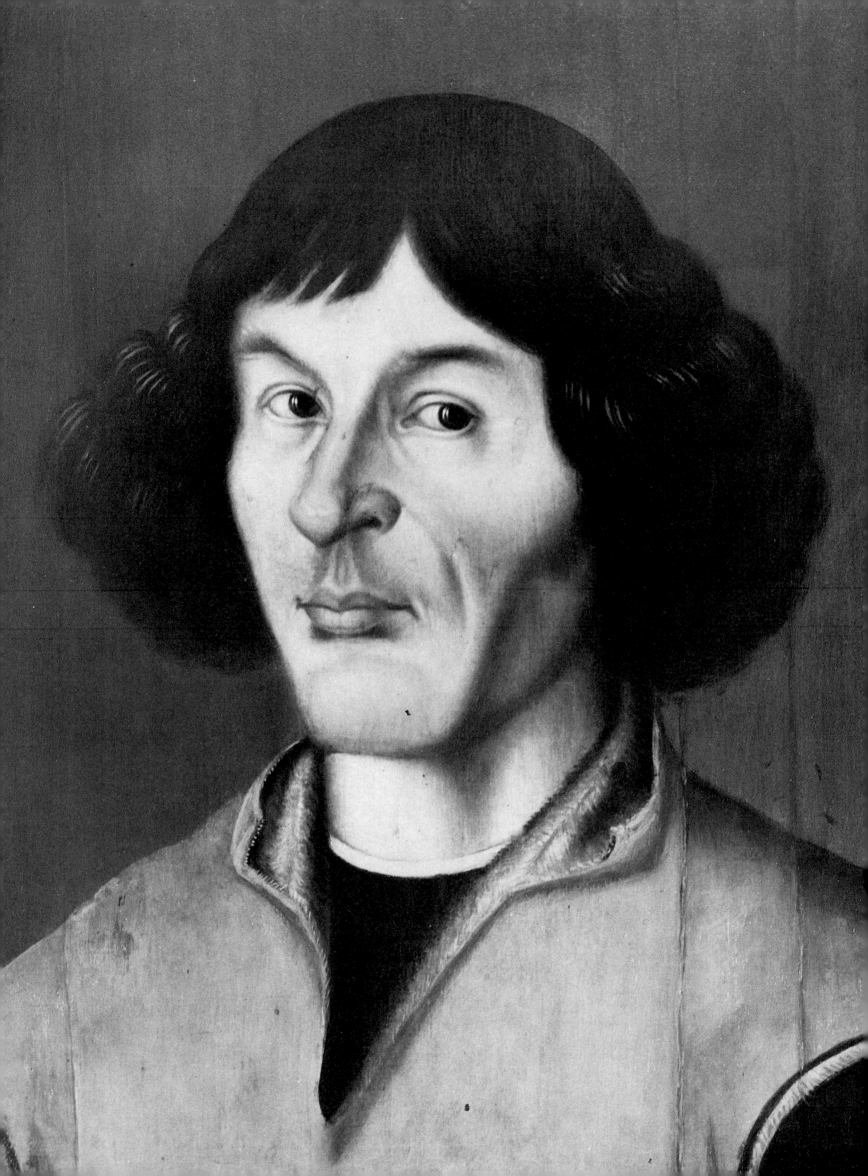

UNKNOWN CRACOW PAINTER (EARLY 16TH CENT.)

Battle of Orsza, details

NATIONAL MUSEUM IN WARSAW

In the early 16th century, bound by its union with Lithuania, Poland took part in the war between Muscovy and Lithuania caused by a conflict over Ruthenian lands conquered earlier by the Lithuanians.

This oldest battle scene in Polish painting shows the battle of Orsza, waged on 8 September 1514 between the Polish-Lithuanian and Muscovite forces. In this battle the Polish-Lithuanian armies under the command of Prince Konstanty Ostrogski, Grand Hetman of Lithuania (c. 1460—1530), won a great victory over Muscovy.

This painting standing "on the boundary between painting and cartography and reconnaissance and military documentary" (Stanisław Herbst) is a striking documentation of detail in weaponry, human types — treated as portraits — as well as of the topography of the battle site stretching out over areas of land intersected by the rivers Dniepr and Orszyca. It is very likely that the painter was an eyewitness to the event.

42

43

MARCELLO BACCIARELLI (1731—1818)

The Prussian Homage

NATIONAL MUSEUM IN WARSAW

We are more familiar with Matejko's portrayal of this event, with the renaissance splendour of Cracow's Market Square, the Clothiers' Hall and St. Mary's church, with the blue sky of a fine, spring day. We are also familiar with the unexpectedly sulky expression on the face of the cunning court jester-Matejko, deep in thought about the future fate of the country.

The event took place on 10 April 1525, when the Prussian Prince Albert Hohenzollern, the former Grand Master of the Teutonic Order which had just been dissolved, swore an oath of allegiance to Sigismund I, the king of Poland. The union, formed from the territories of the former Order, was the beginning of the formidable Prussia, which together with Russia and Austria carried out the first partition of Poland in 1772.

This less well-known work of Bacciarelli is one of a series of historical paintings commissioned by Stanislaus Augustus Poniatowski, and was intended for the Knights' Hall in the Royal Castle in Warsaw.

44

HENRYK RODAKOWSKI (1823—94)

The War of the Hens

NATIONAL MUSEUM IN WARSAW

In 1537 the nobility, assembled in a levée-en-masse against the Moldavian Wallachians, rebelled — for the first time in Polish history — against King Sigismund (I) the Old and his Queen Bona. The nobility demanded that legislation and the treasury be put in order, that Bona be stopped redeeming mortgaged royal lands, and called for the return of royal estates illegally distributed among the magnates.

The rebellion — contemptuously dubbed "the War of the Hens" from the great number of hens eaten by the rebels — was headed by Mikołaj Taszycki, Jan Sierakowski and Piotr and Marcin Zborowski, all of them rather vague and inconsistent in their actions. The king confirmed earlier privileges including the one which deemed that nothing could be resolved without the consent of the nobility, and soon all the rebels dispersed quietly to their homes.

The painting by Rodakowski — known chiefly as a prolific portraitist — depicts the scene of the reading out of the list of royal privileges (a plain concession on the part of the king) by Hetman Tarnowski on the castle terrace in Lvov. In the middle there is a group of courtiers gathered round King Sigismund the Old and Queen Bona.

45

JAN MATEJKO (1838—93)

The Hanging of the Sigismund Bell at the Cathedral Tower in Cracow in 1521

NATIONAL MUSEUM IN WARSAW

The Sigismund Bell, known as "Sigismund", was cast in Cracow in 1520 at the bell foundry of Hans Beham of Nuremberg and was installed in the Wawel tower in honour of King Sigismund the Old. This bell has become a major national symbol and to this day has been used to announce important and joyful events. It also rings at times of sorrow and suffering.

Matejko's painting shows the moment of the hanging of the bell and the ceremony of its consecration in the presence of King Sigismund and his court, in a pageant of rich attire, opulent fabrics, gold chains and gems. This painting portrays the heyday of Sigismund's "golden age" with its affluent stability expressed in hieratical, official poses, serious and dignified expressions and lofty gestures. The effect is one of somewhat grandiose pomposity, which is offset with healthy vitality by the restless, vibrant and lively other part of the painting depicting artisans at work. It has to be borne in mind that Matejko painted his picture at a time when the robustness and strength of the common people was already coming to mean something more than mere picturesqueness.

Stańczyk, Sigismund's court jester — as always a *porte parole* of Matejko himself — is sitting on the edge of the two groups, of the courtiers and the workers, and is mockingly imitating the workers. Yet he is also apprehensive as if perceiving in their stern, tense faces some threat to the decaying structures concealed behind still splendid façades.

We present the whole painting and detail.

KAROL MILLER (1835—1920)

Jan Kochanowski and Chancellor Zamoyski at Czarnolas

JAN KOCHANOWSKI MUSEUM AT CZARNOLAS, LOAN BY THE NATIONAL MUSEUM IN CRACOW

Jan Kochanowski (1530—84), the greatest poet before Mickiewicz, the creator of Polish literary language, spent what were probably his happiest years far from the intrigues of the court, in the rustic refuge of Czarnolas. There he wrote, among other things, *The Dismissal of the Greek Envoys, Sobótka* and *Threnodies* which were inspired by the death of his beloved daughter Urszulka, the only painful event to overshadow the blissful period at Czarnolas.

As a friend of Kochanowski, Jan Zamoyski (1542—1605), the Grand Hetman of the Crown and prominent statesman during the rule of Stephen Báthory, tried to win the poet's favours for the king and make him use his excellent penmanship for the needs of what would be termed today the state propaganda. The tragedy *The Dismissal of the Greek Envoys,* full of allusions to contemporary state affairs, was written to commemorate the wedding of Jan

Zamoyski and Krystyna Radziwiłł, and was staged on 12 January 1578 at Ujazdów. The performance was graced by the presence of the royal couple.

The last words of the tragedy "... let us advise each other on war, let's not only be on the defence/let's take counsel about how and whom to fight, rather than wait for the foe", sounded like a specially coined political slogan, all the more so since the wedding was attended by senators and envoys who during the coming session of the Seym were to arrive at a decision on the war against Muscovy.

Zamoyski used to visit the poet at Czarnolas when hunting nearby, and on such occasions Kochanowski dedicated several verses to him.

Jan Kochanowski (1530—84), poet, humanist, leading representative of the Polish Renaissance.
Detail of tombstone at church in Zwoleń; circa 1610

JAN MATEJKO (1838—93)

The Union of Lublin

CASTLE IN LUBLIN,
LOAN OF THE
NATIONAL MUSEUM IN WARSAW

The union between Poland and Lithuania — known as the Union of Lublin — was concluded at the Seym in Lublin on 28 June 1569. Henceforth there was to be one Seym, one king, jointly elected, and foreign policy binding both states. On the other hand the treasuries, government offices and armed forces were to remain separate. The Polish-Lithuanian Union, inspired chiefly by the Polish nobility, brought about the policy of eastward expansion

which later, on more than one occasion, gave rise to serious conflicts.

Matejko's painting, which commemorated the 300th anniversary of this event, is rather less evocative than *Skarga's Sermon* or *Rejtan*. The central group with King Sigismund Augustus holding the crucifix aloft is perhaps too theatrical, and so is the royal box with the paper-like figure of Anna the Jagiellon, copied from an old portrait. On the other hand the full-blooded Lithuanian magnates (as a rule in opposition to the union) are splendid, and the faces of Prince Mikołaj Radziwiłł (kneeling with a sabre) and Cardinal Hosius (sitting on the left with his hands raised) are extraordinarily beautifully modelled.

The introduction by Matejko of Andrzej Frycz Modrzewski into the picture is full of significance. Modrzewski, a distinguished political theorist and writer, is shown embracing a humble peasant (on the extreme right). Modrzewski was one of the first Poles to condemn the oppression of peasants.

"These two characters, joined as brothers by a cordial handshake," writes Juliusz Starzyński, "... are of special importance for us today: we can see in them not so much the hope for a just reign, but rather a reproach for and a warning against the danger of the licence of dynastic and magnate interests governing the country."

We present the whole painting and detail.

50

JÓZEF SIMMLER (1823—68)
The Death of Barbara Radziwiłł
NATIONAL MUSEUM IN WARSAW

The private lives of rulers have always been a source of inspiration in the arts and literature. Love affairs, marriages and marital infidelities, and mysterious intrigues have always held a particular attraction for artists and writers.

Sigismund Augustus married his second wife Barbara secretly. She was the daughter of Jerzy Radziwiłł, the Grand Hetman of Lithuania, and widow of the Novgorod Voivod Gasztołd. Later, when Sigismund succeeded his father to the throne and admitted to the marriage, his mother Bona Sforza and the Seym demanded that it be broken off as unworthy of a king (Sigismund's first wife, Elizabeth, and his third — Barbara's successor — Catherine were the daughters of an emperor). The king, who loved Barbara dearly, threatened to abdicate, but later, having strengthened his position through the alliance with the Habsburgs, brought his wife to Cracow, and in 1550 had her crowned Queen of Poland.

Soon after the coronation Barbara died — as legend has it, poisoned by Bona — and the disconsolate widowed king accompanied her remains as far as Vilna, where she was to be interred. He went on horseback, and when passing towns and villages would dismount from his horse and follow the coffin on foot.

Alojzy Feliński and Stanisław Wyspiański based plays on this romantic love affair, and besides Simmler, who painted several versions of Barbara's death, the subject was also taken up by Matejko.

Barbara Radziwiłł (1520—51), second wife of Sigismund Augustus. Miniature from a series of portraits of the Jagiellons made in the studio of Lucas Cranach the Younger, second half of the 16th century. National Museum in Cracow, Czartoryski Collections

Sigismund Augustus (1520—72), king of Poland (crowned in 1548), last ruler of the Jagiellonian dynasty. Miniature from a series of portraits of the Jagiellons made in the studio of Lucas Cranach the Younger, second half of the 16th century. National Museum in Cracow, Czartoryski Collections

ARTUR GROTTGER (1837—67)

Henry of Valois Fleeing Poland

NATIONAL MUSEUM IN WARSAW

Done in a romantic convention this painting by Grottger depicts the night escape of the first elective king of Poland, Henry of Valois (1551—89). Elected by the Seym in 1573, he stayed in Poland only a few months; on 18 June 1574, on receiving news of the death of his brother Charles IX, he fled Cracow to become Henry III of France.

In Poland he felt ill at ease and was not popular. An outstanding French poet, Philippe Desportes, accompanying the king to Cracow, wrote an unpleasant squib on Poland, to which Jan Kochanowski retorted with a Latin verse *Gallo crocitanti*.

JAN MATEJKO (1838—93)

Báthory at Pskov

NATIONAL MUSEUM IN WARSAW

An incident from the Polish-Muscovite war for Livonia, conducted in the years 1578—82 by Stephen Báthory, became the subject of the painting which "belongs to the greatest artistic achievements of Matejko both in its force of expression and exquisite harmony of composition, and the beauty of colour" (Juliusz Starzyński). It is not often that this painter is so highly evaluated from the artistic point of view.

From a war studded with Polish military successes Matejko chose a particular moment and place: the period of final negotiations leading to the conclusion of peace, and the foreground of Pskov, the town-bastion besieged by Báthory for several months during the harsh Russian winter.

Neither the battle itself, nor the spectacular victory, but the diplomatic game, the mutual weighing up of arguments — in short, the whole mechanism of great politics — are revealed in this painting, the true drama of which consists in the faces of but a few protagonists: the king, Chancellor Jan Zamoyski, the papal legate, Jesuit Possevin, and the Polotsk ruler Cyprian who offers Báthory bread and salt. Both the face and countenance of the king show pride, even arrogance, yet at the same time dignified concentration; the face of Zamoyski (standing behind the king) reflects alert tension, as if self-confidence was combined here with caution; Possevin — with the face of a model diplomat — is full of cunning astuteness, whereas the face of the splendidly dressed Polotsk ruler shows the dignity and melancholy of the loser who nevertheless believes in the victory of his arguments.

The war between Báthory and Ivan the Terrible ended on 15 January 1582 with a truce at Yam Zapolski whereby Poland gained Livonia and returned her latest conquests, including Velikiye Luki, to Russia.

UNKNOWN ARTIST

Battle of Oliwa (Battle at Gdańsk Port in 1627) etching from the diary of A. Boote

VOIVODSHIP STATE ARCHIVE IN GDAŃSK

Polish armed forces on the Baltic had won a certain importance as early as the 15th century (The Thirteen Years' War with the Teutonic Knights). Expanded later (as the so-called privateers' fleet) by Sigismund the Old, Sigismund Augustus and Stephen Báthory, the Polish navy thrived at the time of the Vasas who — helped by Jan Weyher, voivod of Malbork and Chełmno — formed an impressive fleet, its chief bases being situated at the ports of Gdańsk, Puck and Władysławowo. From 1626 the fleet, administered by the Royal Maritime Commission, was under the command of Admiral Arend Dickmann. It was under his leadership that on 27 November 1627 the Polish navy, armed with a strong artillery, defeated the Swedes at Oliwa, thus lifting the blockade of Gdańsk.

This etching, showing a sea battle at the entrance to Gdańsk Port, comes from the diary of A. Boote, Dutch legate to Poland in the years 1627-28.

JAN KRIEG (c. 1590—c.1643)

View of Gdańsk

NATIONAL MUSEUM IN GDAŃSK

Gdańsk, a major port situated on the Vistula estuary, played an important role in the grain trade which in the 16th century contributed significantly to the general prosperity of the Commonwealth. Under the Vasas in the 17th century the town flourished as did its baroque architecture, art (especially painting) and its rich culture.

The painting by Krieg shows the view of the town from the grounds of a fine suburban residence at Biskupia Górka Hill, where an elegant company has just gathered. Two riders in Polish attire can be seen proceeding toward the town from the direction of the villa. We present the whole painting and detail.

JAN SZWEDKOWSKI (1809—?)

The Homage
of the Shuyski Tsars

MUSEUM OF ART IN ŁÓDŹ

In the first half of the 17th century Poland took advantage of internal turmoil in Muscovy and started a war which was full of spectacular episodes such as the brilliant Polish victory at Kłuszyno (1610), the capture of Smolensk, and the entry of Hetman Stanisław Żółkiewski into Moscow. These successes gave rise to the illusory idea that Muscovy could be united with Poland under the rule of Sigismund III Vasa whose ambition was to sit on the Kremlin throne.

In Moscow Żółkiewski took captive Vasili IV Shuyski with his brothers Dmitri and Ivan and brought them back to Warsaw where at the Seym convened on 27 September 1611 they appeared before the king.

The Polish garrison left behind in Moscow was soon forced to leave the town and the boyars' growing resistance to Poland, as well as their placing upon the throne a new tsar from the Romanov family, dispersed Poland's illusions as regards reigning over Muscovy.

Łukasz Opaliński (1574—1654), castellan of Poznań, in the years 1634—50 Grand Marshal of the Crown, portrayed with a marshal's staff with royal initials, a symbol of his high post.
This portrait is a perfect example of a formal representation of a Polish noble; unknown artist, c. 1640, National Museum in Cracow, Czartoryski Collections

VISC
SIE

JAN MATEJKO (1838—93)

Skarga's Sermon

NATIONAL MUSEUM IN WARSAW

"No Pole has ever painted anything like this," wrote a contemporary critic (Stanisław Tarnowski) about *Skarga's Sermon*. Indeed this work by the 26-year-old artist fully reveals his unusual — rarely observed in other historical painters — vision of history perceived as a cruel mechanism of causes and effects, as a tragic wheel in perpetual motion which lifts nations up and brings about their downfall.

60

Matejko's picture is not so much historical as historiosophical, giving as it does a thorough analysis of past events and their impact on the future.

In the splendid nave of Wawel Cathedral, a Jesuit preacher Piotr Skarga (1536—1612) tells his congregation (including King Sigismund III Vasa) of future national misfortunes. In the centre is a group of three magnate firebrands led by Michał Zebrzydowski, the organizer of a rebellion against the king. It was defenders like these of the ill-conceived "golden freedom" who were later to bring about the downfall of the Poles.

"You will be left not only without a ruler... but also without your fatherland and kingdom, miserable exiles, despised everywhere, poor vagrants...," wrote Piotr Skarga in a draft for one of his speeches to the Seym, incidentally never delivered in this version.

In *Rejtan* painted two years later the three rebels will turn into three national traitors, and in *Poland in Fetters* (1863), the third sequel to this painful triptych, the traitors will be replaced by tsarist hangmen enfettering the captive nation, while the august interior of the Wawel shrine will be transformed into a blood stained ruin.

ISAAK VAN DEN BLOCKE (d. 1628)

Apotheosis of Gdańsk's Links with Poland
painting on the ceiling of the Red Room, details

MAIN TOWN HALL IN GDAŃSK

This allegorical painting in Gdańsk Town Hall takes as its subject the indissoluble bond of Gdańsk with Poland, the bond which became the basis of the economic flourishing of this Baltic port in the 16th and 17th centuries.

The artist presented a panorama of Gdańsk with a familiar silhouette of the Church of Our Lady, on the magnificent triumphal gate which forms the foreground of the composition. The White Eagle is rising up over the town, and the hand of Providence can be seen emerging from the Heaven over the Town Hall. A symbolic rainbow links the source of the Vistula (ships carrying grain can be seen on the river — detail of the painting below) with the Baltic.

At the foot of the picture, amidst the crowd of town patricians, a burgher of Gdańsk and a Polish magnate are seen shaking hands solemnly.

WITOLD PIWNICKI (1851—?)

Stanisław Żółkiewski at Cecora

NATIONAL MUSEUM IN CRACOW

The death of Stanisław Żółkiewski (1547—1620), Grand Hetman of the Crown, is a good illustration of the popular, old soldierly motto *Dulce est pro Patria pugnare* (Sweet it is to fight for one's country). In 1620 the victorious commander in the battle of Kłuszyno (1610, on the river Moscow) with the Muscovite armies found himself in Moldavia, this time to fight the Turks. In the hard, ill-fated battle at Cecora, the 73-year-old hetman showed unusual valour. Having lost his arm, he went on fighting although the situation was becoming increasingly hopeless. Making his retreat — still fighting — he fell. Żółkiewski's severed head was sent by the Turks to Istanbul, whence his widow bought it back and buried it in the family grave at Żółkiew. It was by that grave that the young John Sobieski took his first lessons in patriotism, later to avenge the Cecora defeat as the conqueror of the Turks in victorious battles at Chocim, Vienna and Parkany.

63

UNKNOWN PAULITE PAINTER
(SECOND HALF OF THE 17TH
CENT.)

The Siege of the Paulite Monastery at Jasna Góra in 1655 by the Swedish Army under General Burchard Müller

PAULITE MONASTERY
AT JASNA GÓRA IN CZĘSTOCHOWA

The Swedish "deluge", which descended on Poland in 1655 as a result of a disgraceful agreement between the invader and part of the Polish artistocracy was a real tragedy for the Commonwealth. The Swedish armies occupied nearly the whole country — from the Baltic to the mountains — ravaging and looting the towns and settlements on the way. Dozens of newly built edifices, baroque mansions and churches, were left smouldering ruins; and huge estates with their magnificent works of art were plundered mercilessly by the occupying forces.

It was irregular military detachments, organized throughout the country chiefly by Hetman Stefan Czarniecki, and comprising the noblemen, townsmen and peasants, which finally chased the Swedish troops of Charles Gustavus out of Poland.

The defence of the Paulite Monastery at Jasna Góra in Częstochowa undertaken by the monks, townsfolk and peasants under the command of the prior Augustyn Kordecki (1603—93) was of enormous moral significance for the captive nation. The siege of Jasna Góra by General Müller's troops lasted from 18 November till 26 December 1655 and was successfully resisted by the Poles. Kordecki himself left a vivid account of the siege, which gave rise to a colourful legend drawn upon in a most evocative way by Henryk Sienkiewicz in his novel *Potop* (*The Deluge*).

Stefan Czarniecki (1599—1665), soldier, celebrated commander, Field Hetman of the Crown.
Detail of a portrait painted by Brodero Matthisen (d. 1666). National Museum in Warsaw, Royal Castle

HENRYK PILLATI (1832—94)

The Swedes in Poland

MUSEUM OF ART IN ŁÓDŹ

The Swedes occupying Poland between 1655 and 1657 were notorious for their cruelty towards the civilian population. They burned castles and humble abodes alike, plundered works of art and private property, armed reiters frequently looting peasant farms in search of food.

There has been a recurring pattern of such events in Polish history and it would be possible to collect a large number of paintings showing the invader's violence, from the German and Tartar incursions in the Middle Ages to the Nazi aggression of our own times.

LEOPOLD LOEFFLER (1830—98)

The Death of Czarniecki

NATIONAL MUSEUM IN WROCŁAW

As depicted by the 19th century painter, the death of Hetman Stefan Czarniecki, hero of the Swedish wars, creates a sentimental impression in primer-book style.

The aged leader is dying, surrounded by a retinue of loyal soldiers who have brought in his faithful horse in full battle array.

Stefan Czarniecki (1599—1665), Field Hetman of the Crown, is one of the favourite national heroes, often to be found in the 19th century iconography along with Prince Joseph Poniatowski and General Thaddeus Kosciuszko.

67

BERNARDO BELLOTTO CALLED
CANALETTO (1721—80)
Jerzy Ossoliński
Entering Rome in 1633
NATIONAL MUSEUM IN WROCŁAW

The splendour of the former
Commonwealth would be especially
in evidence on grand, official occasions
such as coronations, funerals, and
ceremonial arrivals, when the most
opulent of costumes were worn,
horses were groomed festively,
and appropriate decorations were put
up. Apparently, the magnificence
of all such occasions was surpassed
in 1633, when on a mission to Pope
Urban VIII Jerzy Ossoliński, the
Grand Chancellor of the Crown,
adviser to King Ladislaus IV Vasa,
was entering Rome. The Polish
delegation impressed Europe with
its incredible wealth almost Byzantine
in its sumptuousness, exotic, semi-
oriental attire, hussar wings and,
allegedly, real gold on the hooves of
the horses "accidentally" lost on the
way from Piazza del Popolo to the
Vatican.

JÓZEF BRANDT (1841-1915)

Lassoing

NATIONAL MUSEUM IN POZNAŃ

"How many battles were fought there, how many people – no one had counted and no one remembered. Only the eagles, hawks and ravens knew, and whoever heard from afar their cawing and the flutter of their wings, whoever saw them swirling and circling over some spot – guessed that it was there that dead bodies and bones were lying unburied... In the long grass men were hunted as if they were wolves or antelopes. And anybody who felt like it hunted."

This description of the Wild Fields – a part of the Ukraine situated far in the south-eastern borderlands of the Commonwealth – which opens Henryk Sienkiewicz's novel *With Fire and Sword*, recalls one of the cruellest wars which the Poles were fated to fight. This was the war against the rebellious Cossacks, marked by many bloody encounters (Zoltye Vody and Korsun, 1648) and one tremendous victory at Berestechko in 1651 where the Polish troops were commanded by King John Casimir. The war "had irreversible consequences and its after-effects were just as tragic for Poland as for the Ukraine (Michał Tymowski, Jan Kieniewicz and Jerzy Holzer, *Historia Polski*, 1987).

Józef Brandt's picture, painted with panache in a romantic spirit, takes us to the wide-open steppes where one of those numerous skirmishes described by Sienkiewicz is being fought. Jan Matejko's painting on the other hand depicts a real event which took place on 8 October 1648. On that day the leader of the rebel Cossack forces, Bohdan Khmelnitski or Chmielnicki (c. 1595-1657) together with his ally from the Tartar Horde, Tuhai Bei, stopped at the walls of Lvov and laid siege to the city. Lvov fought back and finally the Cossacks withdrew, some said thanks to the miraculous intervention of the Blessed John of Dukla whom Matejko shows floating on a cloud. Perhaps the Cossack bandore-player (shown in the lower part of the picture), his hands covered in blood , is singing a mournful *dumka* about all those horrible, strange and miraculous events.

JAN MATEJKO (1838-1893)

Khmelnitski
and Tuhai Bei at Lvov

NATIONAL MUSEUM IN WARSAW

UNKNOWN PAINTER (TURN OF THE 17TH AND 18TH CENT.,
PERHAPS JAN VAN HUCHTENBURG; 1647—1733)

Battle of Chocim

STATE ART COLLECTIONS AT WAWEL

The victorious battle of Chocim in November 1673 brought fame to Hetman John Sobieski and contributed considerably to his election (crowned in 1674). The picture, painted later, probably as late as after the battle of Vienna (1683) — Sobieski's greatest success — is in a way a glorification; however, it faithfully reconstructs the topographical background (the Dnester and the castle) and contemporary costume.

John III Sobieski (1629—96), king of Poland (crowned in 1674), one of the most outstanding Polish military commanders.
Detail of a portrait by an unknown painter, end of 17th century, Palace in Wilanów

UNKNOWN PAINTER (LATE 17TH CENT.)

John III Sobieski at Vienna

NATIONAL MUSEUM IN CRACOW, CZARTORYSKI COLLECTIONS

The battle of Vienna, perhaps the most famous one in which a Polish soldier took part, waged on 12 September 1683 between the western European armies and the Turks, boasts rich iconographical documentation. The struggle between 70,000 combined Polish, Austrian and German forces (including over 21,000 Poles), headed by John III Sobieski, and 70,000 Turks under the Grand Vizier Kara Mustafa is portrayed in full baroque richness; armour, horses, camels, banners and tents are scattered over a broad background which is framed by a view of the town with the characteristic spire of St. Stephen's Cathedral. Such paintings, usually commissioned (most notable were those by Altomonti and hanging in the church at Żółkiew), greatly propagated the military success which brought an end to the century long Turkish expansion in Europe.

The paintings which originated in John Sobieski's own milieu focused on the person of the commander-in-chief and as a rule tended towards a pompous glorification whereby the king — dressed in splendid Roman armour — was presented as an allegory of Fame, blowing a gold trumpet and trampling a Turkish prisoner with his mounted horse.

This less well-known painting from the Czartoryski Collections is perhaps more chronicle-like in its manner than other representations; it records faithfully details of the king's attire: a blue *kontush* overcoat with split sleeves and white silk *zhupan* as well as a pointed fur cap with a heron feather — exactly as the king described them in a letter to his Queen Marie. In his letter John III thus estimated the victory at Vienna: "Our Lord and God blessed of all ages has brought unheard of victory and glory to our nation. All cannon, the whole camp, untold riches have fallen into our hands. Having covered the trenches with corpses the enemy now flees in confusion."

John III Entering Vienna

NATIONAL MUSEUM IN WROCŁAW

Executed on the 200th anniversary of the relief of Vienna this imposing water colour by Juliusz Kossak, known also as *The Triumph of John III,* shows Sobieski entering Vienna the day after the victorious battle which saved the town from the Turkish invasion. Sobieski himself thus describes this event in a letter to his consort Marie Casimire:

"Today I was in the town which could not have lasted more than five days... The common people kissed my hands, feet and dress; others only touched me exclaiming, 'O, let us kiss this hand so valiant!' "

JÓZEF BRANDT (1841—1915)

King John III and Queen Marie Casimire on an Outing from Wilanów

NATIONAL MUSEUM IN WARSAW

Dynamic battle scenes, skirmishes with Tartars and Swedes, galloping horses, billowy banners, and dazzling abundance of war booty are favourite motifs in "baroque" pictures by Józef Brandt, a leading 19th century Polish historical painter.

This depiction of a winter outing by the royal couple from their favourite residence, Wilanów, testifies to the artist's feeling for the flavour of the Sarmatian epoch, with its colourful customs, splendid balls, sleigh rides, and hunts, for which the virile king had such a liking.

UNKNOWN 17TH CENTURY PAINTER

Elections at Wola near Warsaw, details

STATE ART COLLECTIONS AT WAWEL

After Sigismund Augustus, the last of the Jagiellons, had died without heirs in 1572, kings were elected during what was known as a free election, at an assembly of the nobility which usually took place at Wola near Warsaw. The noblemen — each had the right to vote in person — would gather in Warsaw to report at the election field, in their respective voivodship sections. In the middle of the field, in an enormous royal tent the senate would be in session, counting up the votes collected by the deputies. The first free election took place in April 1573 when Henry of Valois was elected king. Other monarchs were elected in a similar manner, including Stephen Báthory, Augustus (III) the Saxon and Stanislaus Augustus Poniatowski.

The Wawel painting probably records the election in 1697 of Prince de Conti who — though elected by a majority vote — was never crowned king.

80

BERNARDO BELLOTTO
CALLED CANALETTO
(1721—80)

Krakowskie Przedmieście Street with the Sigismund Column
Długa Street
Krakowskie Przedmieście Street from the Cracow Gate (detail)
Miodowa Street (detail)

NATIONAL MUSEUM IN WARSAW

The Venetian painter known in Poland as Canaletto, who in 1767 was employed by King Stanislaus Augustus Poniatowski, recorded on canvas various views of Warsaw in the second half of the 18th century with photographic faithfulness to detail. This faithfulness in depicting architecture proved extremely useful after World War II when his paintings served as documentary records during the rebuilding of Warsaw from the destruction wrought by the Nazis.

Canaletto shows Warsaw bustling with life, its streets crowded with carriages and people of various estates in the course of their various daily occupations. This life and movement is evidence of the great vitality of this beautiful northern city which at that time was often admired by foreigners.

JÓZEF CHEŁMOŃSKI (1849—1914)

Casimir Pulaski at Częstochowa

NATIONAL MUSEUM IN WARSAW

Before he died in distant America, during the siege of Savannah, Pulaski's valour brought him fame in his native Poland where he was a leading participant in the Bar Confederacy (1768—72), established in defiance of the king and Russia. First Pulaski distinguished himself in the defence of Berdyczów, then, having covered many a mile, he found himself with his detachment at Częstochowa (1770). There he took the monastery at Jasna Góra and for a long time valiantly resisted repeated attacks by Russian troops, organizing brave raids.

In 1772 (first partition of Poland) Pulaski left the country and after several attempts at organizing Polish detachments abroad he went on to America.

Józef Chełmoński, an unrivalled pictorial interpreter of the Polish character and of nostalgic climes in the eastern border lands, as well as an unsurpassed master in depicting unbridled foursomes, did not draw upon historical themes often, but here too, he was able to leave a mark with his great skills.

STANISŁAW BATOWSKI-KACZOR (1866—1946)

Casimir Pulaski at Savannah

CASIMIR PULASKI MUSEUM AT WINIARY NEAR WARKA

Poles have frequently taken part in the struggle for the freedom and independence of other nations: Thaddeus Kosciuszko and Casimir Pulaski, for example, won fame in the American War of Independence; Józef Bem and Henryk Dembiński fought in Hungary during the Revolution of 1848/49 and Ludwik Mierosławski at the same time participated in the struggle for the freedom of Italy.

Casimir Pulaski, regarded today as a national hero of the United States, found himself in 1777 in America, where at the head of a legion he himself had organized, he won numerous successes, including the victorious battle at Charleston (1779). He died on 9 October 1779 during the siege of Savannah, Georgia.

83

JAN MATEJKO (1838—93)

Rejtan

NATIONAL MUSEUM IN WARSAW

The shameful partition agreement
under the provisions of which Prussia,
Russia and Austria divided among
themselves part of Polish territory
was ratified by the Polish Seym

convened at the Royal Castle
in Warsaw on 21 April 1773.

This tragic event became the
subject of a striking painting by
Matejko, perhaps his best. It
reconstructs the high treason: the
three Poles — Szczęsny Potocki,
Adam Poniński and Ksawery
Branicki — are about to enter the
Senate Hall in order to put their
signatures to the humiliating documents.
They are barred entrance by Tadeusz

Rejtan, deputy of Novgorod, who has prostrated himself in a vain attempt at stopping them.

The rest of the Poles with King Stanislaus Augustus, who has left his throne and now is standing with a watch in his hand deep in thought and helpless, cluster tightly in a corner of the room. Above them, on the balcony, Prince Repnin, the Russian ambassador, has taken a seat. The castle room is a pitiful sight

with chipped stucco work, curtains torn, brackets broken, candles burnt out; the floor is littered with scattered papers, and a chair lies overturned. A coin — perhaps one of Judas' silver pieces, which has fallen out of Poniński's pocket — is dangling ominously on the edge. In the middle, on the wall reigns a portrait of the Empress Catherine II.

It seems that Matejko's painting, a symbolic image of the collapsing

Commonwealth, is the middle section in a triptych which also includes *Skarga's Sermon* and *Poland in Fetters* (1863). The first shows how the then still strong state structure is beginning to show cracks due to internal conflicts (Zebrzydowski Rebellion), while the other portrays the national suffering brought about by dissension and betrayals taken advantage of by the foe. We present the whole painting and detail.

JAN MATEJKO (1838—93)
Rejtan, detail
NATIONAL MUSEUM IN WARSAW

Stanisław Staszic (1755—1826), clergyman, philosopher, political and civic leader at the time of the Four Year Seym (defended the interests of the townsfolk and peasants), writer, scholar and organizer of academic life in Poland (from 1808 president of the Society of the Friends of Learning), prominent geologist, pioneer of the Polish mining industry.
A steel engraving by Antoni Oleszczyński (1794—1879), National Library in Warsaw

KAZIMIERZ WOJNIAKOWSKI (1772—1812)

Proclamation of the May 3rd Constitution, 1791 (Four Year Seym Session)

NATIONAL MUSEUM IN WARSAW

The progressive constitution, known as the Constitution of 3rd May, drafted by enlightened Poles and genuine patriots, was one of the last attempts at saving the fatherland. This modern constitution, the second after that of the United States to formulate principles of government, was soon to be abolished by the treacherous Russian-incited Confederacy of Targowica.

The solemn occasion of the proclamation of the law, which took place in a stately room at Warsaw Castle, was a frequent theme in paintings and drawings among which Jean Pierre Norblin's and Kazimierz Wojniakowski's versions stand out.

MARCELLO BACCIARELLI (1731—1818)

Portrait of Stanislaus Augustus with an Hour Glass

NATIONAL MUSEUM IN WARSAW

Stanislaus Augustus Poniatowski (1732—98), the last King of Poland, continues to arouse the emotions of historians and journalists, for it is very difficult to pass an equivocal judgment on his role in Polish history; he was a proponent of reform and co-author of the May 3rd Constitution, but also a member of the Targowica Confederacy which led to the abrogation of the reforms passed by the Four Year Seym and to the second partition of Poland.

This allegorical portrait of Stanislaus Augustus was painted in the spring of 1793 and soon afterwards the king left for Grodno to take part in a session of the Seym which confirmed the second partition of Poland. The painting, the detailed composition of which was elaborated by the king himself (the storm raging outside the window, the globe, the hour glass, state documents and the royal crown put aside), was captioned with the Latin inscription "Quaesivit coelo lucem", taken from Virgil's *Aeneid,* and was to convey the drama of the situation in which the king and Poland found themselves in the face of imminent disaster.

It seems, however, that in this attractive painting by Bacciarelli (the king kept ordering more copies which he readily gave away) there is something artificial, something of the false pathos of an actor playing a tragic part but not being fully aware of its implications.

89

MICHAŁ STACHOWICZ (1768—1825)

Thaddeus Kosciuszko Taking an Oath at Cracow's Market Square

NATIONAL MUSEUM IN CRACOW

After the abolition of the May 3rd Constitution, and the second partition of Poland by Prussia and Russia, a national rising broke out, led by Thaddeus Kosciuszko. Kosciuszko (1746—1817), who had distinguished himself in the American War of Independence, was appointed Supreme Military Commander of the National Armed Forces on 24 March 1794 and with his sabre raised pledged on Cracow's Market Square that he would "chase away the three potentates" (Mickiewicz).

The participants in the insurrection included the peasants who were promised personal freedom and the easing of labour dues.

The motif of Kosciuszko's Allegiance is one of the most popular in Polish national iconography and has been exploited countless times in various forms, both in official professional art and in primitive and folk renditions.

Thaddeus Kosciuszko (1746—1817), national hero, illustrious soldier and military engineer, worthy participant in the American War of Independence (1775—83), commander-in-chief of the insurrection in 1794.
An etching based on a portrait by Józef Grassi, c. 1794

90

ALEKSANDER ORŁOWSKI
(1777—1832)

Battle of Racławice

NATIONAL MUSEUM IN CRACOW,
CZARTORYSKI COLLECTIONS

Aleksander Orłowski was one
of the first Polish painters to show
a penchant for native themes. As
a young apprentice in Jean Pierre
Norblin's studio, he left everything
to join the Kosciuszko Insurrection.
On the battlefield, he sketched the
peasant scythebearers and the
Commander, later using these
sketches in his well-known
presentation of the battle of Racławice
(4 April 1794). This painting records
the scythebearers' attack on the
Russian battery which ensured
Kosciuszko's victory.

JEAN PIERRE NORBLIN DE LA GOURDAINE (1745—1830)

Street Skirmishes in Warsaw

NATIONAL MUSEUM IN WARSAW

Jean Pierre Norblin, a French painter brought over to Poland by the Czartoryski family, at first did indifferent courtly scenes in the rococo manner of Watteau, but later became interested in the Polish way of life, in types of noblemen, townsmen, peasants and Jews. He portrayed them and their customs mainly in drawings thus introducing, in a way, a Polish trend into his work. At the time of the Four Year Seym, the proclamation of the May 3rd Constitution and in particular during the stormy days of the Kosciuszko Insurrection, he made sketches of what was going on in the streets of Warsaw. His series of documentary drawings constitutes an eyewitness account of these events, striking even today in its authenticity. This is a drawing depicting a street battle in Warsaw during the Kosciuszko Insurrection.

UNKNOWN PAINTER (END OF
THE 18TH CENT.)

Hanging the Effigies
of Traitors

NATIONAL MUSEUM IN WARSAW

During the Kosciuszko Insurrection,
public executions of traitors, the
members of the Targowica
Confederacy, were carried out at the
instigation of the radical wing of the
revolutionary Polish Jacobins.

Some of the traitors, including
Hetman Piotr Ożarowski and
Bishop Józef Kossakowski, were
indeed hanged, while others, those
who managed to escape, including
Ksawery Branicki, Szczęsny Potocki
and Seweryn Rzewuski, were later
executed in effigy, their portraits
hanged on the gallows.

This cruel scene, reconstructed
by an unknown artist from the Norblin
circle, is being observed by a leading
Polish Jacobin, probably Jakub
Jasiński, standing by with a raised sabre.

ALEKSANDER ORŁOWSKI (1777—1832)

The Slaughter of Praga

NATIONAL MUSEUM IN CRACOW, CZARTORYSKI COLLECTIONS

The exceptionally bloody storming
of the right-bank district of
Warsaw, Praga — on 4 November
1794 — by tsarist troops commanded
by General Suvorov, put an end to the
Kosciuszko Insurrection. The civilian
population was not spared and the war —
as shown by Orłowski — literally
rolled over people's dwellings to an
accompaniment of "children's groans
and mothers' crying" (Mickiewicz).

In his reconstruction of this painful
incident Orłowski with amazing
perception anticipated the haunting
atmosphere of Picasso's *Guernica*
which was inspired by the events of
the Spanish civil war of 1936.

95

JANUARY SUCHODOLSKI (1797—1875)

General Henryk Dąbrowski Entering Rome at the Head of His Legion

NATIONAL MUSEUM IN WARSAW

General Henryk Dąbrowski (1755—1818) won fame chiefly as the founder of the Polish legions in Italy (Milan, 9 January 1797), the first Polish armed movement during the time of the partitions.

In 1797—1803 the legions fought on the side of France and the allied Italian states against the Austrian, Neapolitan and Russian troops.

Suchodolski's painting shows the legions entering Rome through the Porta del Popolo. The event took place on 3 May 1798. According to Józef Drzewiecki, one of the participants, "the day was most beautiful, with the Italian sun shining and windows adorned with elegant women; we marched in columns up the Capitol Hill".

96

JÓZEF SONNTAG (1784—1834)

Kozietulski Leading the Third Light-cavalry Regiment in the Somosierra Ravine

NATIONAL MUSEUM IN WARSAW

The eight-minute charge of the Polish light-cavalry commanded by Jan Kozietulski (1781—1821) at the Somosierra pass in the Guadarrama mountains on 30 November 1808. smashed the last bastion of Spanish resistance thus opening the way for Napoleon to Madrid. The Poles took all the guns, banners and prisoners;
however it is a pity that this brilliant victory was won on foreign soil, and in the struggle against a free nation which the Emperor of the French had decided to conquer.

PIOTR MICHAŁOWSKI (1800—55)
Somosierra
NATIONAL MUSEUM IN CRACOW

This battle scene by Piotr Michałowski, undoubtedly the most outstanding Polish artist of the early 19th century, is remarkable not only because of his mastery of the medium.

A Romantic dash in applying the paint, and swift strokes of the brush which leave aggressive streaks on the canvas, form so dynamic a composition that at first glance it is difficult to tell what it is portraying. Soon however silhouettes of horses and navy blue and raspberry-red uniforms of famous cavalrymen breaking through the smoke and greyish Spanish hills can be distinguished. The lightning charge recedes into the background of the painting. A slanting shaft of light defies all rules of classic harmony.

Michałowski had a different vision of the Somosierra charge from that of Sonntag and managed to recapture the very essence of the battle. Employing the purest artistic devices he achieved a striking effect, powerfully suited to a gallant fight in the Napoleonic style.

We present the whole painting and detail.

MARCELLO BACCIARELLI
(1731—1818)

Napoleon Granting a Constitution to the Duchy of Warsaw, sketch for a painting intended for the Royal Castle in Warsaw

NATIONAL MUSEUM IN WARSAW

One of the longest lasting legends in Polish history is that of Napoleon. The Poles having finally lost independence in 1795 placed their hopes in Bonaparte. At that time he was gaining increasing fame, first as the commander of the revolutionary French army in Italy, then successively as the consul of the Republic and finally, from 1804, as the Emperor of the French who, fighting Poland's enemies, scored one victory after another. The Polish legions in Italy, the uprising in Great Poland in 1806 and the Duchy of Warsaw (1807) are all closely associated with Napoleon.

It was thanks to Napoleon that the Polish soldier fought with hope again, first in foreign lands, and later, after 1807, also on Polish soil, in the army of the Duchy of Warsaw. The cult of Napoleon was immense and the atmosphere accompanying the approach of his armies — perhaps best evoked in the final books of Mickiewicz's *Pan Tadeusz* — full of elation.

The retreat from Moscow was a bitter disillusion, yet the legend has survived and has become a source of inspiration for innumerable poems, songs, tales and paintings.

This painting by Bacciarelli shows the creation by Napoleon of an independent duchy formed from patches of liberated Polish lands.

The Duchy of Warsaw, created by Napoleon under the provisions of the Treaty of Tilsit in 1807, and abolished in 1815, was granted a Constitution. The event took place on 22 July 1807 in Dresden, whenceforth the Saxon Frederick Augustus I, having been nominated Duke of Warsaw, was to reign over the Duchy with varying fortunes.

The Constitution, based on the Napoleonic Code, proclaimed that all citizens were equal before the law, abolished serfdom and made Polish the official language.

The scene portrayed by Bacciarelli in fact never took place for it was not from the hands of the Emperor himself that Stanisław Małachowski, Józef Wybicki and Wincenty Sobolewski, shown in the painting, received the document. We present the whole painting and detail, a portrait of Napoleon.

HENRYK PILLATI (1832—94)
The Death of Berek Joselewicz at Kock
NATIONAL MUSEUM IN WARSAW

Berek Joselewicz (1764—1809), who was a Jewish merchant and colonel in the Polish army, took part in many campaigns and battles in defence of Polish independence.

He organized a Jewish light cavalry regiment to fight in the Kosciuszko Insurrection of 1794, was an officer in the legions formed in Italy by Jan Henryk Dąbrowski, and from 1807 fought in the army of the Duchy of Warsaw, and was killed in the battle against the Austrians at Kock.

JANUARY SUCHODOLSKI (1797—1875)

The Death of Cyprian Godebski at Raszyn

NATIONAL MUSEUM IN WARSAW

Cyprian Godebski (1765—1809), poet, participant in the Kosciuszko Insurrection and valiant soldier in the Polish legions in Italy, was killed on 19 April 1809 in the battle of Raszyn, waged against the Austrian army by the detachments of the Duchy of Warsaw commanded by Prince Joseph Poniatowski.

January Suchodolski, a pupil and follower of Horace Vernet, portrays the well-known scene of a commander bidding a dying soldier farewell. One is tempted to put into Prince Joseph's mouth the words of Napoleon when one of his favourite marshals was dying: "Why am I not allowed to cry?"

103

UNKNOWN ARTIST (EARLY
19TH CENT.)

Temple of Sibyl at Puławy

NATIONAL MUSEUM IN CRACOW,
CZARTORYSKI COLLECTIONS

In the early 19th century, Puławy
was one of the main centres of Polishness. Princess Izabela Czartoryska
founded the first Polish museum there
(Temple of Sibyl, 1801, and the Gothic
House, 1809) in which, apart from
works of art, she amassed numerous
mementoes of Polish kings, hetmans,
national leaders, as well as
contemporary personalities such as
Thaddeus Kosciuszko and Prince
Joseph Poniatowski.

These mementoes were displayed
chiefly in the Temple of Sibyl, the
entrance of which bore an appropriate
inscription, "The Past to the Future",
meaning that the national heritage
collected here was to survive — as
in Noah's ark — the deluge of the
partitions, and be handed down to
future generations.

The round building standing in the
Puławy park, on the high bank of the
Vistula, spread hope all over the
country until as late as the outbreak
of the November Uprising (1830), when
Puławy had to be evacuated in the
face of imminent threat. After many
years of making do with temporary
shelters the collections finally found
permanent refuge in Cracow in 1876.

UNKNOWN ARTIST

Polish Soldiers
at Puławy in 1809

NATIONAL MUSEUM IN CRACOW,
CZARTORYSKI COLLECTIONS

Especially during the Napoleonic
wars the Temple of Sibyl, the national
pantheon of the Poles in Puławy,
attracted Polish soldiers, who flocked

here to donate their war trophies and
put their signatures in special
memorial books.

In 1809 after the victorious
campaign of the Duchy of Warsaw
against Austria, many wounded
soldiers turned up at Puławy where
they were offered assistance. This
drawing commemorating these events
and captioned by Izabela Czartoryska
herself, was kept at the Temple of
Sibyl.

Izabela Princess
Czartoryska née Fleming

(1746—1835), founder of a museum in
Puławy. Detail of a painting executed
by an unknown French artist in 1774,
National Museum in Cracow

UNKNOWN PAINTER, AFTER HORACE VERNET

The Death of Prince Joseph Poniatowski at the Battle of Leipzig

POLISH ARMY MUSEUM IN WARSAW

Prince Joseph Poniatowski (1763—1813) had a long apprenticeship before becoming part of national legend as one of its chief protagonists. Trained as a soldier in Austria, he fought with distinction in the victorious battle of Zieleńce (1792). Having taken part in the Insurrection of 1794 he withdrew from public life after his uncle Stanislaus Augustus Poniatowski joined the Targowica Confederacy.

After a few years of idleness — during which he was often to shock public opinion with his controversial behaviour — Prince Joseph joined Napoleon in the hope that the Emperor of the French would help Poland regain independence. As the commander-in-chief of the army of the Duchy of Warsaw, formed by Napoleon in 1807, he distinguished himself in the campaigns of 1809 and 1812.

His end came in the famous Battle of the Nations at Leipzig, on 19 October 1813 where he drowned together with his horse in the river Elster. Prince Joseph's body (recovered from the river) was soon after laid to rest in the royal crypt at Wawel, while his sabre and spurs found their way to the Temple of Sibyl at Puławy.

The painting by the popular French painter Horace Vernet recording the heroic death of this Marshal of France (the title conferred on Poniatowski by Napoleon in 1813) gave rise to a long series of copies and imitations made throughout the 19th century, often very primitive and devoid of any artistic value.

JAN NEPOMUCEN BIZAŃSKI (1804—78)

The Raising of the Kosciuszko Mound

NATIONAL MUSEUM IN CRACOW

This painting by Bizański portrays a broad cross-section of people of Cracow who in 1821 built this unusual monument to honour the victor of Racławice.

The gathering includes the prosperous bourgeoisie and urban poor, elegant society ladies and students, and noblemen, wearing *kontush* topcoats to manifest their patriotism for the occasion, are also in abundance. Everyone felt obliged to bring a barrow full of earth to the site which was marked with a tall pole. The Commander himself — presented in a baroque manner among fleecy little clouds — is looking down from the heavens.

At the time of the partitions, especially in Cracow, similar patriotic demonstrations were often organized; Polish national anniversaries provided excuses for festivities, and chapels were erected to commemorate national heroes among whom Kosciuszko and Prince Joseph Poniatowski were most revered.

107

WINCENTY KASPRZYCKI (1802—49)

Fine Arts
Exhibition in Warsaw in 1828

NATIONAL MUSEUM IN WARSAW

The years immediately preceding
the November Uprising of 1830
brought a remarkable flowering
of culture and the arts in Warsaw;
the Neo-classical-cum-Romantic
edifice of the Grand Theatre was
erected, Chopin wrote his early
compositions, and young painters
from the Fine Arts Faculty of Warsaw
University acquired their skills,
participated in contests and exhibited
their works to the public.

One of these young artists,
Wincenty Kasprzycki, portrayed with
photographic accuracy the interior
of a university hall where in 1828,
amongst others, the painters Marcin
Zaleski and Antoni Brodowski
(seated right) exhibited their pictures.
Among those shown in the painting
is also the author himself.

MARCIN ZALESKI (1796—1877)
Seizing of the Arsenal
NATIONAL MUSEUM IN WARSAW

The November Uprising against Russia — one of the first bids for freedom — began during the night of 29 November 1830. After the November Night, in which a major role was played by students from the Cadets' School, difficult months followed full of military engagements, successes alternated with defeats.

The unprecedented dash and courage of the young patriots were in effect wasted due to the inefficiency and indecision of successive chief commanders. The pacification of Warsaw carried out by the Viceroy Paskevitch's troops at the beginning of 1931 after nearly 10 months of fighting put an end to the hopes of November.

In the rather modest iconography pertaining to the November Uprising a few paintings by Marcin Zaleski, an eyewitness of these events, stand out. Executed with meticulous care they faithfully portray various familiar spots in Warsaw (Zaleski was noted for his cityscapes) and what was going on there, including the bringing of prisoners to the town together with banners taken in victorious battles at Wawer and Iganie, as well as the return of Polish detachments from Wierzbno.

The seizing of the Warsaw Arsenal on the night of 29 November 1830 is presented as if from a distance, on a broad plane. Devoid of pathos and exaltation the cool detachment of the painting suggests a press photo.

WOJCIECH KOSSAK (1857—1942)

Olszynka Grochowska

POLISH ARMY MUSEUM IN WARSAW

One of the harshest battles of the November Uprising was waged in the Warsaw suburb of Grochów, or more precisely at Olszynka Grochowska on 25 February 1831. Polish troops commanded by General Józef Chłopicki fought against the Russian army under General Dybich. As a result of this bloody but inconclusive battle some 17,000 soldiers were killed or seriously wounded, including over seven thousand Poles.

Wojciech Kossak, son of Juliusz (the outstanding painter of historical and genre scenes), in his numerous, highly competent and still very popular paintings created a lively vision of the Napoleonic epic and the November Uprising.

WOJCIECH KOSSAK (1857—1942)

Sowiński on the Ramparts of Wola

POLISH ARMY MUSEUM IN WARSAW

The heroic death of Józef Sowiński (1777—1831), the general with a wooden leg (he lost a leg in 1812 in the battle of Borodino) took place on 6 September 1831 on the ramparts of Wola, in the last battle of the November Uprising, during the bloody storming of Warsaw by Russian troops headed by General Paskevitch.

The gallant soldier, commemorated in a poem by Słowacki, is a popular hero of Polish poetry and patriotic songs and is also frequently portrayed in drawings and paintings.

Julian Ursyn Niemcewicz (1758—1841), poet, author of popular *Śpiewy historyczne* (Historical Songs, 1816) — a history of Poland in rhyme, which served as a history textbook for a few generations of Poles; also a soldier, Kosciuszko's aide-de-camp, emigré activist, died abroad.

Detail of a painting by Antoine Jean Gros (1771—1835), National Museum in Cracow, Czartoryski Collections

Frédéric Chopin (1810—1849), the greatest Polish Romantic composer whose music, the evocation of the Polish national character, has become part of the world's artistic heritage
Detail of a copy made by Stanisław Stattler of the portrait painted by Ary Scheffer (1795—1858), National Museum in Cracow, Czartoryski Collections

TEOFIL ANTONI KWIATKOWSKI (1809—91)

Ball at the Hôtel Lambert in Paris (Chopin's Polonaise)

NATIONAL MUSEUM IN POZNAŃ

Every year the Hôtel Lambert in Paris — one of the main centres of the Great Emigration after the November Uprising, the residence of the Czartoryski family — opened its premises for splendid balls, the proceeds of which went to refugees from Poland.

Teofil Kwiatkowski, an excellent though still underestimated artist,

executed a series of paintings
referring to this event. His are not
documentary pictures, but poetic
transformations, visionary projections,
in which participants of some
patriotic masquerade turn round and
round to the sound of Chopin's
music. Noblemen in traditional
attire mingle here with winged
hussars, the mediaeval knight

Zawisza the Black, the poet Adam
Mickiewicz, the Czartoryski family,
Chopin, and a barefoot girl with a braid
transplanted to Paris straight from
a Masovian field. The statue-like
Prince Adam Czartoryski, regarded by
one faction of emigrés as the national
leader and future king of Poland, can
be seen making his way — as if half
asleep — through those dancing.

The painting by Kwiatkowski is
one of the first national pageants in
Polish art; languid, lethargic and
hopeless, this turning round and round
is a *sui generis* prologue to Jacek
Malczewski's *Melancholy* (see p. 148).
and to the famous finale of Stanisław
Wyspiański's drama *The Wedding*.
We present the whole painting and
detail.

117

JULIUSZ KOSSAK (1824—99)

Adam Mickiewicz with Sadyk Pasha in Turkey

NATIONAL MUSEUM IN POZNAŃ

The greatest Polish poet and national bard Adam Mickiewicz having published *Pan Tadeusz* in Paris in 1834, to all intents and purposes gave up poetry and became involved in political activity aimed at serving the cause of freedom and democracy among the peoples of Europe. In September 1855 he was in Constantinople in order to explore the possibility of forming Polish legions there to fight Russia. In Turkey, he met Michał Czajkowski (1804—86), a fascinating character; successively a November Uprising participant, emigré in France, and Adam Czartoryski's agent in Turkey, commissioned by the Hôtel Lambert to organize an anti-Russian campaign in the Balkans and Caucasus. Czajkowski, who became a convert to Islam and assumed the name of Sadyk Pasha, entered the Turkish service and on Mickiewicz's initiative organized six legions of Cossacks and Balkan Slavs to fight the Russians. Some years later Sadyk Pasha changed his loyalties, converted to the Orthodox religion, returned to the tsarist service, and finally committed suicide. Mickiewicz died in Constantinople on 26 October 1855, probably of cholera.

Adam Mickiewicz (1798—1855), the greatest Polish Romantic poet, national bard, also involved in politics. Etching from a daguerreotype by Szweycer, 1851, Adam Mickiewicz Museum of Literature in Warsaw

118

ÉDOUARD DEMBOWSKI avec la procession massacré par les autrichiens le 28 Février 1846 à Podgórze (Faubourg de Cracovie)

EDWARD DEMBOWSKI z procesją: napadnięty od austriaków dnia 28 Lutego 1846 na Podgórzu w Krakowie

UNKNOWN ARTIST

Edward Dembowski Leading a Procession at Podgórze

NATIONAL MUSEUM IN CRACOW, CZARTORYSKI COLLECTIONS

Edward Dembowski (1822—46), a revolutionary and democratic leader, propagator of a joint national rising involving all three partition zones and emissary of this plan in Galicia, played a prominent part in the Cracow revolution of 1846. He was killed by an Austrian bullet at Podgórze (now a district of Cracow) on 22 February 1846 when leading a procession whose purpose was to win the support of the peasants.

And it was because of the total incomprehension by the peasants of its aims that the Cracow revolution failed, while the peasants, incited by Austria, became involved in an anti-feudal revolt led by Jakub Szela.

POLIKARP GUMIŃSKI (1820—1907)

Insurrectionists of 1848 in the Prison in Magdeburg

NATIONAL MUSEUM IN POZNAŃ

In Great Poland the revolution of 1848 manifested itself with an armed rising. When the revolution in Berlin broke out, on 18—19 March, the Poznanians formed a National Committee, and Ludwik Mierosławski, on his arrival from Berlin, began to organize military units. They believed that they could strike a common blow against the Russians together with the Germans, but this did not come to fruition, and the uneasy alliance turned into an armed struggle between the two sides. Although there were some successes like the victory at the battles fought at Miłosław and Sokołów, the uprising collapsed on 9 May, and many of the participants, including Mierosławski, found themselves thereafter in German gaols.

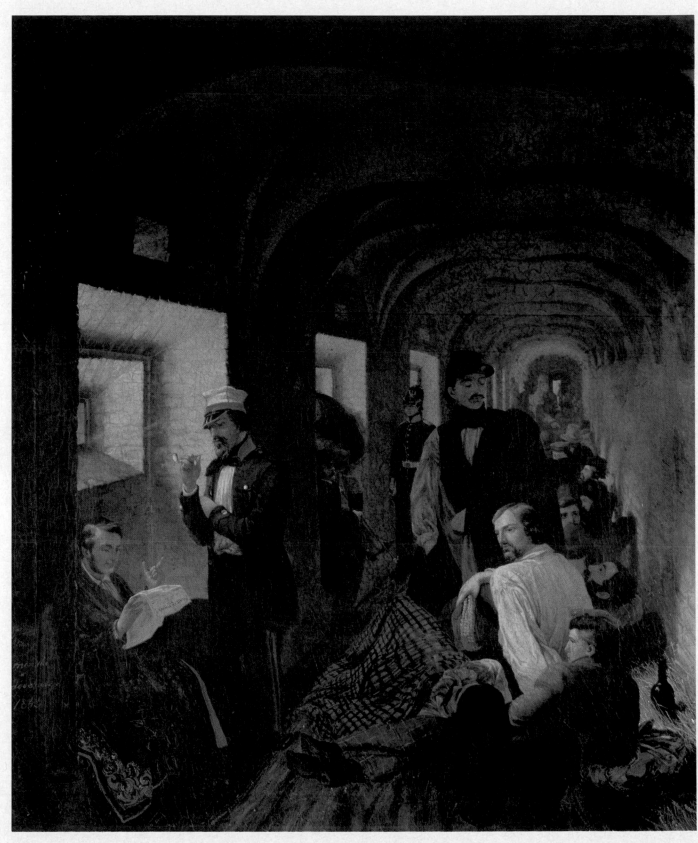

MICHAŁ STACHOWICZ (1768—1825)
Harvest Festival
NATIONAL MUSEUM IN WARSAW

Nineteenth century Polish painters readily drew upon country themes. They were attracted to the picturesqueness of peasant costume and customs, the beauty of peasant types, and the richness of country landscapes changing with the seasons and providing the background for their paintings. Folk themes gained popularity in the Romantic epoch when ethnographic research was begun (Zorian Dołęga Chodakowski, later Oskar Kolberg), and folk music at that time became a source of inspiration to the young Chopin.

In the bucolic atmosphere of the post-harvest time, presented in this charming picture by Stachowicz, the manor and the village co-exist peacefully, the serf enjoying the favours of a just lord.

In the second half of the 19th century this pageant-like treatment of the countryside will give way to more critical narratives of the peasant lot (cf. Aleksander Kotsis' paintings) but even before that happened the brilliant Romantic painter, Piotr Michałowski, in a series of magnificent portraits, had created a genuine image of the Polish people.

122

WOJCIECH KOSSAK (1857—1942)

**The Prussian
Eviction, from
the series The
Prussian Spirit**

DISTRICT MUSEUM IN TORUŃ

After the failure of the revolutionary movements of 1848 in Europe, the might of Prussia was increasingly directed against the Polish inhabitants of Great Poland, Pomerania, and Silesia. Germanisation campaigns intensified in all areas of life, especially after 1862, when Otto von Bismarck became

Prime Minister of Prussia.

After the unification of Germany in 1870, the notorious *Kulturkampf* began: in other words a struggle to "cleanse" German culture of foreign influences This was aimed primarily against the church, and was intended to bring about the complete germanisation of Polish

society. The same aim was also served by the banning of the Polish language from schools and offices (which were mainly staffed by Germans), and by persecuting those who used it. One particularly brutal element in this anti-Polish policy was what was termed the Prussian eviction: that is, the eviction from the Prussian partition zone of those Poles who were not citizens of the German Reich. In the period from 1885 to 1887, about 26,000 Poles were evicted in this way.

Special laws provided the basis for the activities of the Colonisation Commission which purchased holdings from Polish peasants, at first voluntarily and later compulsorily, and handed them over to German colonists. The Poles did not remain passive in the face of these German steps: they repeatedly offered resistance, and were energetic in organising campaigns, particularly in the economic field.

JAN LEWICKI (1802—71)

Galician Slaughter

POLISH ARMY MUSEUM IN WARSAW

The peasant revolution in Galicia in 1846 — the most serious antifeudal movement on Polish territory in the 19th century — coincided with the Cracow uprising in the struggle for liberation. The peasants, ignorant of its aims, were used by the Austrian authorities for paralyzing the uprising.

Bands of peasants led by Jakub Szela invaded the estates and slaughtered their owners. Lewicki's painting, a rare illustration of these painful events, shows peasants carrying the severed heads of their victims to the Austrian authorities.

Portrait of a Peasant Wearing a Hat by Piotr Michałowski (1800—55),
National Museum in Warsaw

126

ARTUR GROTTGER (1837—67)

Farewell to an Insurrectionist
Welcome to an Insurrectionist

NATIONAL MUSEUM IN CRACOW

In Polish national iconography
this painting is of particular
significance. A momentous national
event, the January Uprising, is shown
through the prism of private life, from
the perspective of a manorial homestead.
A wife is saying good-bye to her

husband who is about to leave
to fight for his fatherland.
Dressed in a widow's black dress the
woman is ready to sacrifice her
personal happiness to the national
cause. When the husband returns
defeated (the other part of the diptych)
the wife gives him a cool welcome:
aloof and distant, she is disappointed
in her hopes.

Farewells and welcomes, and
farewells more joyous than welcomes
— this has always been a striking
paradox of the Polish lot.

MAKSYMILIAN GIERYMSKI (1846—74)

Insurgent Patrol

NATIONAL MUSEUM IN WARSAW

This remarkable picture, with its lovingly depicted greys, blues and golds, is one of the most Polish in all our art.

An episode taken from the everyday

routine of the January Uprising — a patrol getting information from a vagrant passing by on a field road — is something like a synthesis of the Polish situation in general.

Being lost in an empty, sandy place, the uncertain waiting for a response to the report of a gun, the search for one's allies and enquiries about the enemy — all this takes on the stamp of absurdity, of hopeless going round and round, of inability to find a way out of the charmed circle. This is an unwitting anticipation of the finale of Wyspiański's drama *The Wedding*.

JACEK MALCZEWSKI (1854—1929)
Death at the Resting Point
NATIONAL MUSEUM IN POZNAŃ

Jacek Malczewski, though he himself had never been to Siberia, conceived a most evocative and penetrating vision of it: a striking and at the same time strangely beautiful picture of the martyrdom of Poles in the snows of distant Russia.

Malczewski was guided by Juliusz Słowacki's *Anhelli,* a mystical poem which was the source of inspiration for his most beautiful, haunting paintings (the series *The Death of Ellenai).*

Death at the Resting Point belongs to another group of Siberian paintings, more realistic in approach, "documentary", as it were, based chiefly on the accounts of Polish deportees after their return from hard labour, the first of whom had been sent to Siberia after the failure of the Bar Confederacy.

The painting depicts the interior of a hut where some convicts have stopped for a short rest having covered another stage of the journey. One of them, a young boy, has just died, and his two companions, deep in thought, keep vigil at his death bed.

Beneath the silent and serene twilight of this painting lies a powerful charge of expression, a mounting pain and anger which must be restrained in the face of the omnipotent guards, but which is ready to explode at any moment. This painting seems to portray the state of the Polish soul in those tragic days.

Jan Matejko (1838—93), painter of historical scenes. His art made a strong impact on generations of Poles who derived their faith in surviving the period of servitude from these paintings, and reflected on the complicated history of their country.
Detail of a self-portrait painted a year before the artist's death, National Museum in Warsaw

UNKNOWN ARTIST, AFTER A DRAWING BY JULIUSZ KOSSAK

The Ceremony of Inauguration
of the Academy of Learning in Cracow

WOODCUT IN THE PERIODICAL *KŁOSY*, NO. 478, 3 JULY 1873

The second half of the 19th century — the era of positivism — witnessed a rapid development of Polish science and culture. In the fragmented country, ruled by the three partitioning powers, Polish scholars managed to build what was a lasting system of scientific research, treating their activity as important, though perhaps not very spectacular, work for the country. This remarkable flourishing of science, matching that of Western Europe, was to bear fruit later when Poland regained its independence.

The expansion of technological, historical and literary research required the constant exchange of experience and also the wide dissemination of its results among society. Thus various Societies of the Friends of Learning came into existence, for example in Poznań (1857) and Toruń (1876), and the Academy of Learning, formed in 187 from the Cracow Scientific Society, was solemnly inaugurated in 1873.

OBCHÓD JUBILEUSZU 50 LETNIEJ DZIALALNOŚCI LITERACKIEJ J. I. KRASZEWSKIEGO. Rysował na drzewie Ksawery Pillati.

KSAWERY PILLATI (1843—1902)

Józef Ignacy Kraszewski's Jubilee in Cracow

ILLUSTRATION IN THE PERIODICAL *TYGODNIK POWSZECHNY*, NO. 45, 5 NOVEMBER 1879

Cultural life with a distinct patriotic flavour thrived especially in Galicia, the most liberal of the three partition zones. The 200th Anniversary of the Relief of Vienna (1883), the 100th Anniversary of the Kosciuszko Insurrection (1894), the 500th Anniversary of the Jagiellonian University, and other national anniversaries gave rise to popular rejoicing. Birth and death anniversaries of great poets (Kochanowski, 1884, Mickiewicz, 1897) were observed in a solemn manner, and funerals of prominent people were held with due ceremony: in 1869 the re-interment of the remains of King Casimir the Great, in 1890 the interment of Adam Mickiewicz's remains brought from Paris, and in 1893 the funeral of Jan Matejko. Monuments, including the statue of Mickiewicz, were unveiled with great pomp.

On 5 October 1879, the jubilee of Józef Ignacy Kraszewski provided an excuse for a great patriotic manifestation. Kraszewski (1812—87), who was celebrating five decades of his writing, gained fame as the author of a gigantic series of novels on the history of Poland.

It was during these celebrations that the National Museum in Cracow was installed in the Clothiers' Hall in the middle of the Market Square. This museum is a most exceptional place where several generations of Poles, while admiring paintings by Matejko, Rodakowski, Chełmoński, Gerson and others, have learnt and continue to learn their history and a sense of Polishness.

KAZIMIERZ ALCHIMOWICZ (1840—1916)

Hiring Labourers

NATIONAL MUSEUM IN WARSAW

The realistic painting of the second half of the 19th century recorded, like the literature of that period, various difficult social situations. The peasants' lot was often portrayed, as well as class differences in the countryside, more pronounced after the enfranchisement of the peasants: the emergence of a new social stratum, that of rich peasants, on the one hand, and on the other, the misery of the poor, forced to abandon their homes and seek employment in large farms or in towns where the developing industry created a demand for cheap labour.

ALEKSANDER KOTSIS (1836—77)
The Last Chattel
NATIONAL MUSEUM IN WARSAW

Critical realism in painting manifested itself in the portrayal of extreme cases of human misery resulting from unjust social relations. There appeared paintings which were accusations and called for a response from the public. The extreme poverty of the peasants in Galicia was a frequent subject for observation in the work of Aleksander Kotsis, the leading representative of the realist trend in Polish painting in the late 19th century. Dark huts, extinguished hearths, empty pots and vessels spelt death, illness, and the hopeless vegetation of human beings devoid of the most basic necessities.

The Last Chattel shows the sequestration of a goat, the family's last source of nourishment, and is one of the most striking paintings in this genre.

FÁBRYKA WARSZAWSKA PAPIEROSÓW, TYTONIU I TABAKI POD FIRMĄ „LAFERME".

BRONISŁAW PUC

"La Ferme" Cigarette, Tobacco and Snuff Factory in Warsaw

ILLUSTRATION IN THE PERIODICAL *KŁOSY*, NO. 344, 1872

The rapid development of industry in the Polish territories (especially in the Congress Kingdom) in the second half of the 19th century was reflected in press illustrations recording from day to day the construction of new factories, the growth of transport, and the application of various technological achievements. Painting remained indifferent to technology, and the attention of artists and especially the realists was focused rather on the social repercussions of the mechanization of life. Not a machine but the human being — in conflict with the former — was the subject of the artist's and the writer's interest.

WACŁAW KONIUSZKO (1854—1900)

The Reading of *Czas* at a Workshop (Cobbler's Monday)

NATIONAL MUSEUM IN WARSAW

The nineteenth century was the age of newspapers. Thanks to the press the flow of information was increasingly fast and ever more people from all walks of life could learn about the current events which made headlines in the world.

This painting by a pupil of Matejko shows the perusing of a popular daily, *Czas,* at a cobbler's workshop. For a young apprentice the reading of the paper over his master's shoulder is his whole extra-mural education, a lesson in history, politics and culture, extremely important — despite the conservative character of the paper — for the development of consciousness in the generation which was to live to see the day of Poland's liberation.

Sand-diggers

NATIONAL MUSEUM IN WARSAW

In the second half of the 19th century the attention of realist painters was focused on everyday life, casual passers-by, often working people. Realist painters (e.g. Courbet in France) realized their aims not only through representing the world of the poor and the toilworn, picturesque often as it was, but mainly through placing emphasis on the darkest current social ills: the growing misery of human existence in the capitalist system. Such a programme was connected with nascent ideas of the social equality of classes.

The mellow colours of Aleksander Gierymski's painting do not carry such a sharp message as does the later *Peasant Coffin*. This is rather an objective narrative, presenting a small segment of 19th century Warsaw, with a modern technological note sounded by an iron bridge stealing into the townscape, sand-diggers on the barges, and above them, fashionable Varsovians, a Jew, and soldiers in foreign uniforms, strolling on the embankment. A detached but telling picture.

FELICJAN KOWARSKI (1890—1949)

The Leaders of "Proletariat"

NATIONAL MUSEUM IN WARSAW

This monumental painting, executed towards the end of the artist's life, constitutes an attempt at creating a historical trend in socialist realism. The painting commemorates the glorious tradition of the workers' movement in Poland, the leaders of the International Social Revolutionary Party "Proletariat", the first Polish workers' party, founded by Ludwik Waryński (1856—89) in September 1882.

The party's programme envisaged the overthrow of capitalism and the introduction of socialism, using strikes and political and economic terror as a means of struggle. The arrests and the trial conducted in 1885 in which Pietrusiński, Kunicki, Bardowski and Ossowski were sentenced to death, and Ludwik Waryński to deportation for many years, put an end to the party's activity. Its ideas, however, disseminated through such periodicals as *Proletariat, Przedświt,* and *Walka klas,* did not pass entirely into oblivion; on the contrary, they made a great impact on the formation of the Polish revolutionary movement.

An artist's impression, painted from surviving photographs, depicts (from the left) Feliks Kon, Stanisław Kunicki, Ludwik Waryński, Piotr Bardowski and Jan Pietrusiński.

142

STANISŁAW MASŁOWSKI (1853—1926)

Spring 1905

NATIONAL MUSEUM IN WARSAW

At the first glance, nothing much is happening in this light, impressionist painting, succulent with fresh spring greenery, and depicting Aleje Ujazdowskie, an elegant district full of the mansions and gardens of Warsaw's aristocracy.

A tightly clustered group of riders is slowly making its way along the middle of the avenue. They are Cossacks, and among them — as if especially hidden from the few passers-by — two walking civilians. They are prisoners, perhaps participants in some revolutionary-cum-patriotic street demonstration which has only just been broken up. Such demonstrations were numerous during the stormy years 1905—6 and took place in many towns in the Kingdom of Poland. The tsarist authorities dealt with demonstrators in a very ruthless manner, usually with the help of the same Cossack cavalrymen, who now appear so serene.

Yet agitation was growing with every passing day and involved ever wider circles in an increasingly conscious struggle for human rights, for the rights of the Polish worker. An enormous role in raising this awareness was played by the workers' parties, PPS (Polish Socialist Party) and SDKPiL (Social Democratic Party of the Kingdom of Poland and Lithuania).

143

WITOLD WOJTKIEWICZ (1879—1909)
Street Manifestation in 1905
NATIONAL MUSEUM IN WARSAW

The paintings of Witold Wojtkiewicz, one of the most outstanding Polish painters, imbued with morbid, expressive symbolism, are usually concerned with general, existential matters. The drawing presented here has some affinity with Jacek Malczewski's *Melancholy* which was painted ten years earlier: the artist — the lonely figure on the right — is Wojtkiewicz himself, and the crowd gathering in a street demonstration which is about to descend on the town with revolutionary slogans. Hope and fear are visible on the artist's neurotic face, but it seems that the melancholy spell will be shaken off this time. And his other drawings of the revolution of 1905, including *The Dawn of Freedom,* prove this.

Maria Skłodowska-Curie (1867—1934), great scientist, chemist, author of research in radioactivity and co-discoverer, with her husband Pierre Curie, of polonium and radium, new chemical elements, winner of two Nobel prizes. Detail of a drawing from life made by Paul Renonard in 1910. Maria Curie-Skłodowska Museum in Warsaw

144

STANISŁAW FABIJAŃSKI (1865—1929)
The Funeral of a Striker
MUSEUM OF ART IN ŁÓDŹ

This painting was based on a real event, the death of a worker during a strike manifestation in 1905 in Łódź. The cortège — painted with coarse, dark, careless streaks — is quickly moving across the factory landscape, effectively introducing the climate of increasing social agitation and the growing anger of the oppressed and the hungry. The tsarist soldiers keep order watching the workers in a silence which is full of tension.

This painting is just one step from Lentz's *Strike,* a dramatic representation of a revolutionary workers' revolt.

STANISŁAW LENTZ (1861—1920)
Strike
NATIONAL MUSEUM IN WARSAW

The workers' stubborn faces, clenched fists, their eyes full of scorn for the oppressor, and full of the certainty of victory in a just cause — all this can be discerned in the superb painting by Lentz, concerning the revolutionary riots in 1905. The three workers (with Warsaw electrician Kolasiński in the middle) are composed into a monumental group emanating immense power.

In the whole of Polish painting — and maybe non-Polish too — there is no other equally expressive reflection of the righteous class struggle.

JACEK MALCZEWSKI
(1854—1929)

Melancholy

NATIONAL MUSEUM IN POZNAŃ

Jacek Malczewski painted
Melancholy exactly on the centenary
of the Kosciuszko Insurrection and
only a year before the centenary
of the third partition — the end of

Poland's independence. Both these
facts are reflected in the painting,
on the reverse of which the artist
wrote: "Prologue of a vision/the last
century in Poland — Tout un siècle."
So it is a look back, as it were, from
the vantage point of the turn of the
19th and 20th centuries, at a whole
century passing by in servitude, bitter,
hopeless, full of doubt as to the chances
of finding a way out from a nightmarish
situation. A view shared by the many

148

contemporaries to whom the
painting was addressed.

The hero of the painting is the
artist/painter helpless in the face
of the theme he is about to undertake.
From the canvas, only just touched
with a brush, or rather from the
troubled consciousness of the artist,
an avalanche of characters spills out:
young boys, mature men, old folk.
Scythes and banners aloft, Siberian
cloaks billowing, the crowd is rushing

along to the wide window of
a studio opening onto a clear,
spring landscape. But just before the
window, guarded by the mysterious
black-clad Melancholy, everything
suddenly freezes, dies away, and then
this whole dizzy dance — increasingly
stiff — seems to start again.

In the midst of the whirlpool of
people we can see a poet, a musician
and a painter, whose work seems
wasted in this chaotic cul-de-sac.

In this painting — one of the
most profound and most striking
of the paintings concerned with the
Polish cause — there is much of the
climate of the finale of Wyspiański's
drama *The Wedding,* written a few years
later. Both these works exude a mood
of dejection which too often affected
the Poles and hindered their actions
at the end of the last century.

We present the whole painting and
detail.

149

JACEK MALCZEWSKI
(1854—1929)

Portrait of Józef Piłsudski

NATIONAL MUSEUM IN WARSAW

Józef Piłsudski (1867—1935):
a deportee to Siberia in his youth,
leader of the Polish Socialist Party,
propagator of the armed struggle for
Poland's liberation, founder of the
Strzelec (Rifleman's) paramilitary organization. As the Commander of
the First Brigade of Legions during
World War I he was interned by the
Germans in Magdeburg from July
1917 till 1 November 1918. On 10
November Piłsudski returned to
Warsaw where he played a leading
role in organizing the Polish state,
liberated after 123 years of subjugation.
The first Seym of the reborn Poland
conferred upon him the title of Head
of State in 1919. In 1920 he was
appointed marshal of Poland.

151

WOJCIECH KOSSAK (1857-1942)

Charge at Rokitna

POLISH ARMY MUSEUM IN WARSAW

The famous charge of the Polish legionary cavalry at Rokitna, a village on the border of Austria-Hungary and Russia, took place on 13 June 1915:

"The horses started ... the grey jackets fluttured in the wind, hands gripped hilt-guards tightly, eyes glittered joyfully. So the longed-for moment has come, the moment about which each of us as a child read in history, in novels, in poetry – we are rushing to charge, in a moment we shall run into the enemy, our sabres will glisten over their heads and we shall cut and chop right and left – who cares about bullets, who cares about shots, we, the Polish cavalry, are charging."

This is how the battle was described by one of the participants, Stanisław Rostworowski (quoted after Andrzej Romanowski, "Mit Rokitny", *Znak* 1987). In fact, the Poles were sent to battle by an order that was based on a miscalculation of the strength of the enemy forces; and following the example of their predecessors at Kirholm, Vienna, Somosierra and Ostrołęka, they fought madly; in their desperate charge which lasted some three minutes, the second squadron of the 15th Uhlan regiment lost 63 soldiers killed, eight missing and 33 seriously wounded.

Nevertheless this bloody encounter had a certain influence on the further course of events on the front, and soon after the myth of Rokitna was born. Rokitna, another Somosierra, was extolled in song, poetry and paintings of which Wojciech Kossak's picture (one of the two that he painted on the same subject) is one of the better known ones.

The bodies of the commander of the squadron, Captain Zbigniew Dunin-Wąsowicz, and of the others killed were buried first at the cemetery at Rarańcza and then in 1923 transferred to the Rakowicki cemetery in Cracow, to a special mausoleum decorated with the following inscription:

"Go, tell Poland, thou who passest by, that here obedient to her laws we lie."

LEON WRÓBLEWSKI (1893—1975)

Great Poland Insurgents before the Hotel Bazar in Poznań

NATIONAL MUSEUM IN POZNAŃ

On 26 December 1918, Ignacy Paderewski, virtuoso pianist and composer, future prime minister and active supporter of the cause of independence, arrived in Poznań. He was greeted by the still German-occupied town with an enthusiastic national manifestation. Thus began the Great Poland Uprising which aimed at joining the Great Poland region and the town of Poznań to the reborn Poland. The uprising, which claimed the lives of some 2,000 Polish soldiers, ended in Polish victory. Under the terms of the armistice signed on 16 February 1919 Poznań returned to Poland.

153

STANISŁAW BAGIEŃSKI (1876—1948)

The Disarming of the Germans in Front of the Chief Headquarters at Saxon Square in Warsaw

POLISH ARMY MUSEUM IN WARSAW

The disintegration of the partitioning powers, tsarist Russia, Prussia and Austria, as a result of World War I, which was drawing to an end, brought new hopes for speedy independence after more than a hundred years of servitude.

The still numerous foreign troops garrisoned on Polish territory became increasingly disorganized, their strength weakening, especially in the Austrian partition zone.

In November 1918 in the Congress Kingdom occupied by German troops, the spontaneous disarming of Germans began on the initiative of the Polish Military Organization (the so-called Piłsudski-ites). On the whole the Germans did not resist, and on the arrival in Warsaw on 10 November of Józef Piłsudski who until then had been interned in Magdeburg, an agreement was immediately made as to the evacuation of the German troops. Also the Polish Regency Council, a body established by the occupying powers, on 11 November 1918 handed over complete authority to Piłsudski.

K. WITKOWSKI

Silesian Insurgents Taking an Oath in 1919

MUSEUM IN TARNOWSKIE GÓRY

Towards the end of World War I there emerged the problem of Upper Silesia and its ties with Poland. Some coalition states, including Great Britain, were in favour of Silesia remaining within Germany and this stand brought about the outbreak of an uprising in Silesia (August 1919), its participants supporting Silesia's ties with Poland. The first rising was suppressed by the Germans, and another broke out in August the following year. Besides patriotic national slogans the insurgents also raised social issues, demanding the improvement of the proletarian lot.

In March 1921 a poll was conducted in Silesia, resulting in the defeat of pro-Polish sentiments, and in May 1921 the third Silesian rising started, the most determined one (a hard-fought battle at St. Ann's Mount), resulting in the division of Silesia between Germany and Poland. Poland gained part of Upper Silesia, while the other part and Opole Silesia went to the Germans. This was later to give rise to numerous conflicts.

The amateurish painting reproduced here shows the insurgents taking an oath during the first rising in 1919.

155

STANISŁAW OSOSTOWICZ (1906—39)

The Peasant Epic

MUSEUM OF THE HISTORY OF THE REVOLUTIONARY MOVEMENT IN WARSAW

This diploma painting by Stanisław Osostowicz from the Cracow Academy of Fine Arts refers to the peasant movement and waves of peasant strikes that repeatedly swept Poland in 1919—22 and 1932—35. The large, expressive canvas in sharp colours shows a clash of two masses: the protesters and those who are there to quell their protest. Its unstableness, achieved through pictorial effects, seems to indicate that something is breaking up and conveys a premonition of a powerful explosion of social structures and political orders, of the inevitability of change, which the artist as a left-winger hoped and fought for.

ANTONI ŁYŻWAŃSKI (1904—72)

The Port in Gdynia

NATIONAL MUSEUM IN WARSAW

On 23 September 1922 the Seym passed a decree on the construction of a port in Gdynia, an old fishing village where as early as the 17th century, under Ladislaus IV Vasa, plans were made to build a naval port. It was with great enthusiasm and the energy, typical of a country reborn, that work was started and soon the village was transformed into a modern commercial port and major town. As early as August 1923 the first ship called at Gdynia. At the beginning of World War II Gdynia was an important outpost of resistance, which continued till 19 September 1939.

WOJCIECH KOSSAK (1857-1942)

Polish Cavalry Parade at Cracow's Meadows on 6 October 1933

NATIONAL MUSEUM IN CRACOW

The year 1933, which in the history of Europe is remembered as the date of Hitler's coming to power, saw in Cracow the celebration of the 250th anniversary of the Relief of Vienna, including the last Uhlan parade at which Marshal Józef Piłsudski took the salute held in Cracow's Meadows at the foot of the Kosciuszko Mound. The twelve cavalry regiments that had marched from various parts of Poland to take part in the ceremony, attended by the President of the Republic, Professor

Ignacy Mościcki, were commanded during the parade by General Gustaw Orlicz-Dreszer.

This bustling picture by Wojciech Kossak, the official portraitist of the marshal and the leading eulogist of Poland's power status in 1918-39, shows a galloping light-horse band in the foreground, followed by the 8th Uhlan Regiment under Colonel Mastalerz riding at a trot, and then, far in the background, on a small stand, the characteristic figure of Marshal Józef Piłsudski saluting the troops.

What was he thinking about at that moment, this man who provided such a poetic and at the same time violent page in Polish history? Was it about the romantic legionary battles, the revival and reconstruction of the country which for over a century had been under foreign domination, about Poland's power among the other nations of Europe, or perhaps about the opportunities that had been wasted? Amidst all the blaring of trumpets, the flutter of pennons and the hoof beats, the marshal seems lonely and detached.

After the parade Piłsudski paid tribute to the ashes of John III in the Wawel Cathedral – where less than two years later he would be laid to rest himself amid the most illustrious Poles – and attended a pontifical mass celebrated by Bishop Adam Sapieha; finally he heard a hundred and one gun salute.

MICHAŁ BYLINA (1904—82)
September 1939
NATIONAL MUSEUM IN WARSAW

The attack on Poland by Nazi Germany on 1 September 1939 began World War II. The Polish soldiers fiercely resisted the invaders, fighting alone despite desperate appeals to their Western allies, and therefore bearing the whole brunt of the initial period of the war.

Poland fought longer than any other European country against the Nazis: for 2,078 days, or in other words nearly six years. September 1939 has become a national legend.

This image of September 1939 is one of the best paintings by Michał Bylina, an extraordinarily prolific follower of the 19th century style in historical painting. Instead of showing combat, the artist concentrated on rendering the atmosphere of those clear September nights and of the long treks in search of dispersed units, and captured that melancholy moment of stillness which follows and precedes a battle. The viewer can almost hear the clatter of the horses' harness and the quiet voices of the cavalrymen, and perhaps also a song hummed furtively.

In a moment, the roar of German aircraft and the rumble of bombs will disperse this detachment and a battle will begin, which Bylina depicted in another painting bearing the same title.

ANDRZEJ WRÓBLEWSKI (1927—57)

Partisans

NATIONAL MUSEUM IN WARSAW

The struggle against the invaders was waged by the nation throughout the war and on all fronts. In this struggle an important role was played by partisan units — a resistance movement which harassed the enemy at any time and place. Sabotage, terrorist operations, the derailing of trains carrying troops and arms to the East, and finally regular battles fought by large partisan forces, all contributed considerably to the weakening of the Nazis and brought forward the moment of victory.

There is an abundant photographic documentation of the underground movement, painting however failed to convey an adequate image of its vehemently romantic spirit. Neither was Wróblewski successful here: his monumental canvas seems excessively formal and unreal.

JERZY KRAWCZYK (1921—69)

A Parcel without Worth

MUSEUM OF ART IN ŁÓDŹ

At least 7.2 million people, including 3.5 million Polish citizens, died in Nazi concentration camps during World War II.

It was in protest against the mass extermination of the Jews that the Jewish Fighting Organization, with the cooperation of the Jewish Military Union, began an uprising in the Warsaw ghetto on 19 April 1943.

This metaphorical painting by Jerzy Krawczyk is a tribute to the tragic fate of the Jews, the nation condemned by the Nazis to total annihilation. By means of the shorthand language of modern art the artist conveyed all that the Nazi occupation meant for the Jews: restriction of their rights, forcing them to wear distinguishing marks — the star of David — confinement in closed ghettoes and finally deportations to the death camps where they perished together with millions of people of various other nationalities.

Krzysztof Kamil Baczyński (1921—44), poet, bard of the generation of young fighters born in the 1920s, served in the Home Army, killed on the fourth day of the Warsaw Rising.
Artistic photograph by Jerzy Sabara from a well-known photo of the poet

ANDRZEJ WRÓBLEWSKI
(1927—57)

Execution

NATIONAL MUSEUM IN WARSAW

Andrzej Wróblewski's picture,
painted several years after the war,
seems to be one of the few works
which adequately convey the
atmosphere of those tragic years.
Contrary to the style prevailing at
the time, it is sparing in its use of
make-believe dramatic effects and
theatricality of composition.

Several figures at the wall.
Helplessness. Shock at the
absurdity of death. Just like in
those photos taken by SS-men
during executions to have something
to boast about back home. The
contours are simple, almost schematic,
the paint is applied roughly, brutally,
as if the artist had forgotten about the
requirements of aesthetics. This
picture could well be supplemented
with statistics taken from the daily
reports of the executioners, with
figures about the numbers killed
in Bydgoszcz, Warsaw, Cracow or
Łódź.

MICHAŁ BYLINA (1904—82)

Lenino

POLISH ARMY MUSEUM IN WARSAW

The battle of Lenino in Byelorussia on 12 and 13 October 1943 was the first battle fought by the Polish First "Thaddeus Kosciuszko" Infantry Division under General Zygmunt Berling, formed in the Soviet Union. This division, the nucleus of the Polish People's Army which towards the end of the war numbered over 400,000 men took part in a long military campaign — including the battle of Studzianki, Warsaw, the Pomeranian Wall, Kołobrzeg, Bautzen and Mielnik — ended its battle trail in Berlin in May 1945.

Having forced a crossing of the river Myereya, soldiers of the division, which formed part of the 33rd Soviet Army of the Western Front, captured the village of Polsukho and reached the village of Trygubovo where they were relieved.

166

STEFAN GARWATOWSKI
(b. 1931)

Hill 593: Monte Cassino

POLISH ARMY MUSEUM IN WARSAW

The Polish Army in the West
organized in France and Britain at
the beginning of the war, which took
part in the Battle of Narvik (1940),
Tobruk (1941), in the Battle of
Britain (1940), the Battle of the Atlantic,

in the Battle of Falaise (1944),
in Belgium and Holland (Arnhem
1944), numbered some 200,000
soldiers in all. In 1943 they were in
Italy, distinguishing themselves in the
Battle of Monte Cassino, by captu-
ring Ancona and liberating Bologna.
This was the battle fought by the
Allies for the opening up of the road
to Rome. After three abortive
attempts at forcing through the
strongly manned Gustav Line on the
slopes of the Apennines, on 18 May

1944 the Polish II Corps seized the
key German position on the highest
hill in the area, Monte Cassino, with
its famous Benedictine abbey.
The losses of the II Corps were
considerable: 860 officers and men
killed, 2,822 wounded and 103
missing.

Garwatowski's picture shows one
of the first assaults in the Monte
Cassino operation, the attack of the
Third Division of Carpathian
Riflemen on the rocky hill No. 593.

STANISŁAW TOMASZEWSKI-MIEDZA (b. 1913)

Struggle in Revenge for the Blood Shed by Thousands of Poles

POSTER MUSEUM IN WILANÓW

The Warsaw Rising, which started on 1 August 1944, contributed one of the most tragic pages to the history of Poland. Soldiers of the underground Home Army, with the help of other combat organizations, dared an arch-heroic feat. For 63 days, until the final capitulation on 2 October 1944, they carried on, street by street, house by house, a desperate struggle against the Nazi invaders.

The rising resulted in stunning losses in killed, especially among young people. Their death, only several months before the end of the war, was one of the gravest, unhealed wounds, particularly strongly felt at the time when people started building up a new life.

In those times which did not favour art, the war poster was the only art form to enjoy the privilege of public display. Pasted on the walls, posters turned the city streets into art galleries. The concise artistic form and idiom that the poster employs possessed inestimable force of expression: it enhanced hatred of the enemy, helped take immediate decisions and encouraged resistance. This poster, one of the best designed by Stanisław Tomaszewski-Miedza, appeared in the streets of Warsaw during the Rising, about 10 August. It depicts the hateful swastika being nailed with bayonets to a wall riddled with the bullets of execution squads. This was the sign of the conscience and the moral duty of the tormented nation.

168

MARIAN SZCZERBA (ur. 1929)

Dying City

POLISH ARMY MUSEUM IN WARSAW

Warsaw emerged from the war as a sea of rubble. Hitler condemned the city to physical destruction. He ordered his troops to level it to the ground and erase it from the map of Europe once and for all. Many times Warsaw was ablaze during the last war: first in September 1939 when German bombs dropped on the Royal Castle; during the urpising in the Jewish ghetto in April 1943; in August 1944 during the Warsaw Rising; and finally after the rising when the Nazis perpetrated the brutal crime of murder on the city. According to the *Wielka Encyklopedia Powszechna*, "84 per cent of the city was destroyed, including 90 per cent of industry, 72 per cent of housing, and 90 per cent of cultural institutions and historic monuments. All monuments, libraries and archives with their collections were destroyed. All bridges were blown up and means of communication suffered serious damage."

EDWARD DWURNIK (b. 1943)

Road to the East

NATIONAL MUSEUM IN WARSAW

Poles repeatedly wandered east, sometimes as conquerors but much more often as exiles and deportees. This Polish Golgotha, especially during the last war, is a particularly painful remembrance and until recently its stations – Kozelsk, Ostashkov, Starobelsk and Katyn – could not be mentioned openly. Many Polish family histories have been branded with this fate and the wound is still open.

The *kibitka* (a cart that carried exiles to Siberia), knout, *nakhayka* (whip), *miny* (Siberian mines) and *gulags* – these words are well known to all Poles. From 1767, when Bishop Kajetan Sołtyk of Cracow together with a group of Polish senators was deported to Kaluga on the order of the Russian ambassador Repnin, till 1945, when sixteen leaders of the Polish underground were tried in Moscow on trumped-up charges, whole generations of Poles crossed Russia on their way to Siberia.

Russia was a party to all the partitions of Poland and the Soviet state, by signing a treaty with Nazi Germany on 23/24 August 1939, took part in the invasion of Poland. Polish officers interned at Kozelsk were massacred by the NKVD in the Katyn forest in 1940. This, together with the mass graves of Poles from the Ostashkov and Starobelsk camps discovered after fifty years of official silence on this subject, reveals the extent of the tragedy of Poles and ever more crosses on this Polish way east.

WOJCIECH FANGOR (b. 1923)

January 1945

MUSEUM OF ART IN ŁÓDŹ

Liberation from the long Nazi occupation came from the East and the decimated nation welcomed its arrival with relief and hope.

This scene, painted in the socialist realist style, depicts the first encounter of Poles with the Soviet and Polish troops who brought with them freedom. Such scenes as this one could be seen in many Polish villages and towns in that memorable winter.

But the war was not yet over and the social and political transformations which followed the liberation and took place amidst struggle for the consolidation of new authority would confront the Poles with many difficult problems.

ALEKSANDER KOBZDEJ
(1920—72)

Pass Me a Brick

NATIONAL MUSEUM IN WROCŁAW

As soon as the war was over Poles were faced with the enormous task of raising up the destroyed country from the ruins. Many undertook this work with invigorating hope enhanced by the prospect of political changes. Their enthusiasm was sincere and their commitment knew no bounds.

"The rapid social and cultural advancement of the broad masses of the people called for an art that was capable of establishing contact with those masses," wrote the critic Mieczysław Porębski when he defined the character of new painting, which was to be realistic, simple in form and dealing with such subjects as work, occupational and political training, and sport. However socialist realism, which in the late 1940s and the early 1950s was the style supported by officialdom, did not come up to social expectations and failed to convey an authentic picture of that epoch of large-scale building projects and the beginnings of the new social order. It failed to be accepted because the people sought in art more profound ideas, corresponding to their rapid tempo of development.

Kobzdej's picture, painted in 1950, is one of the most representative paintings in the socialist realist style.

JULIUSZ KRAJEWSKI (b. 1905)

Land to the Peasants

LENIN MUSEUM IN CRACOW

The Manifesto of the Polish National Liberation Committee — the first official document issued by the People's authorities in Poland — contained a programme for fundamental social and political reform. It included provisions for the return of Poland to a frontier on the Odra and wide access to the Baltic, a new doctrine in foreign policy, and the introduction of radical agricultural reform and universal access to education. The Manifesto of the Polish National Liberation Committee, which was formulated by the Polish left-wing camp, together with the law on the nationalization of industry which came two years later, provided the basis for the political system of People's Poland, determining that it should be a popular democratic state which had chosen the socialist path of development.

The agrarian reform provided for in the Manifesto was carried out in 1944—49. It was directed against the great landowning class and introduced the breaking up of the large estates and the distribution of land among landless peasants or small-holders. This revolutionary campaign, carried out in the complicated circumstances of establishing a new political system, was in part intended to compensate ages-old class disadvantages along the lines of socialist ideals. Socialist realist painting eagerly took up this theme.

This painting of Krajewski's, which dates from 1952, has the attributes of a posed document. It is like a newspaper photograph, in which we can find the typical figures of that period: the soldier, the party activist, a young female activist setting about measuring and dividing up the fields. In the background, a thick-set peasant in a hat is watching the surveyors mistrustfully; this is the wealthy *kulak,* a figure treated universally at that time as the embodiment of the most benighted reaction, and frequently mocked in art.

JAN ŚWITKA (b. 1939)

Crowd. Classification. Picture 7

NATIONAL MUSEUM IN CRACOW

Street crowds, each and every one, individuals and community, the people seen *en masse,* full of movement like corpuscles examined under the microscope.

Composed like a newspaper photo or banal shots in a TV news programme, the picture is modern and cool in its sterile purity. But it makes the viewer think, to reflect on this strange portrait of contemporary Poles. Who are they? What do they think? What are they capable of? What do they aim at? Where are they going on this broad street stage?

Descendants of Jagiello, Sobieski, Czartoryski and Kraszewski, and of the peasants painted by Michałowski and the workers from Lentz's pictures. They are the Poles of the 1970s and 1980s suspended between the complex Past and the difficult Present, imprisoned within the mechanism of History which is revolving faster and faster.

Portrait of a Worker painted by Andrzej Feliks Szumigaj (b. 1938), entitled *A Rest*

The series of Polish faces which are interwoven with pictures of Polish history, begins with a royal portrait, and ends with the face of a working man. This is however more than just a portrait of a worker. Szumigaj's painting — which came at the end of the Cracow exhibition "Portraits of Poles" (1979—80) and repeated later in the album of the same title published by Arkady in 1983 — has been used here again as an established and irreplaceable symbol of the thoughtful Pole, who is level-headed in his assessment of both past history and current affairs, and for whom true national pride is the highest force.

Museum of the History of the Revolutionary Movement in Warsaw

JACEK WALTOŚ (b. 1938)

On Both Sides of the Gate: Holy Saturday 1982

NATIONAL MUSEUM IN WROCŁAW

This view of Polish history in painting ends with a work that dates from the first months of the martial law period and is a reference to the shipyard workers' strike in August 1980. Shown for the first time in an exhibition arranged in one of the churches, it once could not be displayed officially. Today the ban on showing it has been lifted and we include it with no further comment, for the events that followed and the present changes in Poland are known well enough.

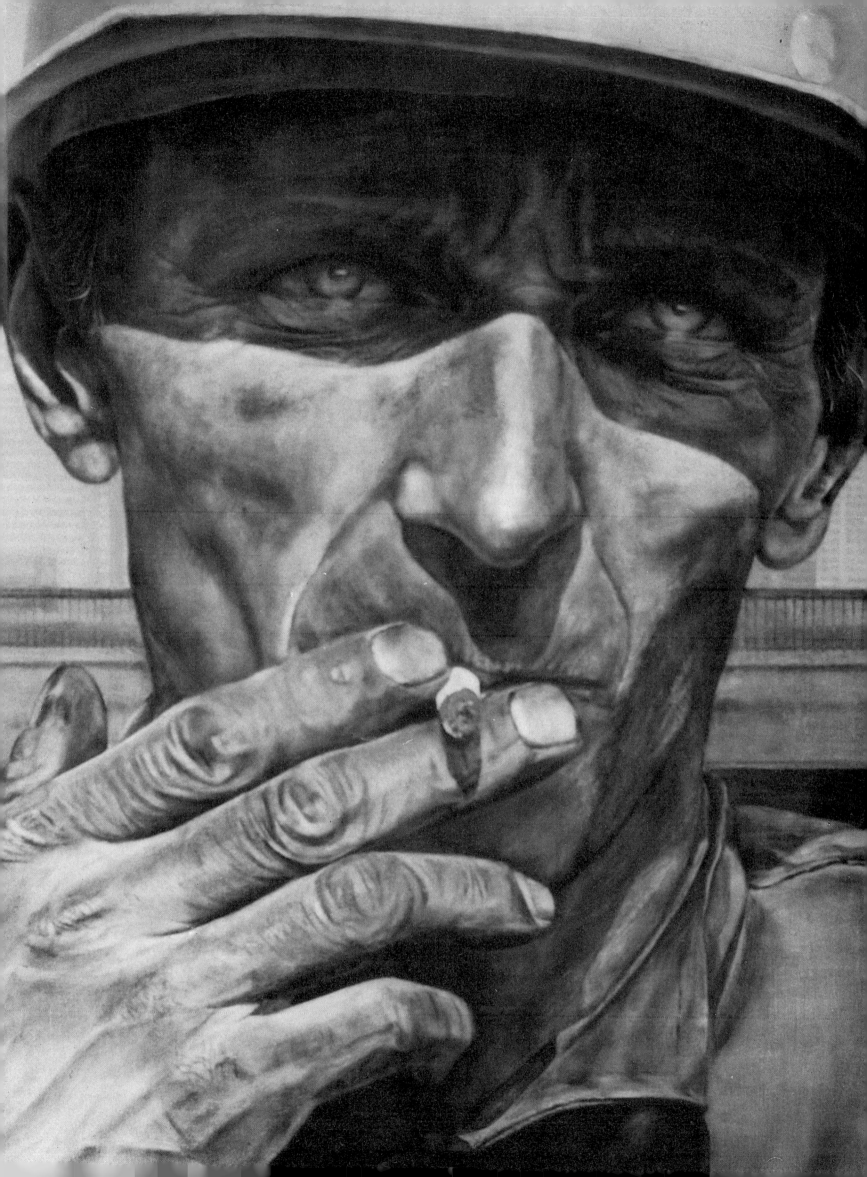